KNITS FOR NERDS

Other books from Joan of Dark

Knockdown Knits

KNITS FOR NERDS

30 Projects:
Science Fiction, Comic Books, Fantasy

JOAN OF DARK
a.k.a. Toni Carr

Andrews McMeel
Publishing, LLC

Kansas City • Sydney • London

Andrews McMeel Publishing, LLC
an Andrews McMeel Universal company
1130 Walnut Street, Kansas City, Missouri 64106.

www.andrewsmcmeel.com

12 13 14 15 16 TEN 10 9 8 7 6 5 4 3 2 1

ISBN: 978-1-4494-0791-9

Library of Congress Control Number: 2011926179

Cover design by Ren-Whei Harn
Page design by Holly Ogden
Photography by Marc Lebryk and Tom Klubens

www.joanofdark.com

ATTENTION: SCHOOLS AND BUSINESSES
Andrews McMeel books are available at quantity discounts with bulk purchase for
educational, business, or sales promotional use. For information, please e-mail the
Andrews McMeel Publishing Special Sales Department:
specialsales@amuniversal.com

: CONTENTS

SECTION_3

COMICS AND MANGA 75

SECTION_4

OTHER STUFF FOR NERDS 97

: ACHNOWLEDGMENTS

This book would not have been possible without the hard work of a lot of people. First and foremost, my agent, Kate Epstein, who would not let a passing comment about a nerdy knitting book pass. My awesome editor, Lane, who has been amazing throughout this process; my tech editor, Ann; and the super talented Holly Ogden at Andrews McMeel, who "got" the design of this book.

Neil Gaiman, for letting a gaggle of roller girls and photographers take over his quiet country home for an entire weekend so the pictures in this book could have an amazing backdrop. And the fabulous Lorraine Garland, who made that weekend happen.

Also, my gorgeous modeling friends, Megan (Dora the Destroyer) Gill, Summer (Jane Ire) Keown, Melia (Kickabroad Crane) White, Ashley (Veronica Dodge) Wilkewitz, Daisy Pignetti, Michelle Markquart and her horse Big Al, Dan (Dill HerO) Carr, Will Hodges, Ray Baxter, Shannon Moore, Chris Pohl, Sarah Emmelman, Lorraine (Quiche MeDeadly) Garland, Michelle Pemberton, Baby Elise, and, of course, Princess the cat.

My incredibly nerdy friend Dylan Roahrig, who knows everything there is to know about *Buffy the Vampire Slayer*. Seriously. Quiz him. A special shout-out to Lorrie Levesque, who had to test-knit an incredibly long scarf!

One of the best parts of this book was working with two of the most talented photographers on the planet, Tom Klubens and Marc Lebryk. Amazing work, guys.

Last, but not least, the designers who helped make this book what it is. I'm proud to have such talented people in my corner.

: INTRODUCTION

I've always been a geek. Growing up with a mom who writes science fiction, a dad who programs computers, and a brother who never met a gifted and talented program he wasn't accepted into, I didn't really have much of a choice! While most kids were packing for summer camp, I was packing for sci-fi conventions with my family. While my girlfriends would swoon over Christian Slater and Leonardo DiCaprio, I had posters of Jonathan Brandis from *seaQuest DSV* and Wil Wheaton from *Star Trek* over my bed.

As a kid, I sometimes tried to hide my nerdiness. But as an adult, I've come to embrace it. I spend most of my day geeking out over books, the newest cell phones, and the latest science fiction series on TV. I love going to sci-fi conventions and seeing the amazing handmade costumes, props, jewelry, and, yes, knitwear that adorn almost every convention goer. It's a haven for not only nerds but crafty people as well!

This book is my gushy love letter to the nerd community. Every pattern is inspired by the things cool kids think are geeky and the geeky people think are cool. Whether you want to give a subtle nod to your rebel love with a girly version of a *Firefly*-inspired Brown Coat, finish off your elf costume with a gorgeous lacy shrug, or cuddle with your very own plush robot, these patterns have something for every kind of nerd!

SECTION_1

FANTASY

: SKILL LEVEL

Intermediate

: FINISHED MEASUREMENTS

92½" (235 cm) long and about 5" (13 cm) wide on lace pattern

: MATERIALS

Patons Silk Bamboo (70% bamboo, 30% silk; 2.20 oz/65 g, 102 yd/93 m): 4 skeins in #85134 Royal (Color A)

DMC embroidery thread: 4 skeins in Metallic Pearl (Color B)

Size 7 (4.5 mm) straight needles

: GAUGE

22 stitches and 20 rows = 4" (10 cm) in Stockinette stitch on size 7 (4.5 mm) needles

ALCHEMY SCARF

: DESIGNED BY TONI CARR

I have a major nerd love for vampire fiction. I have read just about any and every vampire book out there, so it's rare for one to take me by surprise. The YA novel *Vampire Academy* by Richelle Mead did just that. With an awesome twist on the vampire and *dhampir* legends, it really made an impression on me.

The inspiration for this scarf comes from that series. Alchemists use a blend of science and magic to cover up when *dhampirs* hunt the Strigoi, the evil vampires in this world. The alchemists all have gold and shimmering tattoos on their faces that are only visible when they catch the light. Knit in a soft bamboo and silk blend yarn, this scarf features the same hidden tattoos knit in metallic embroidery thread so that the lace flower tattoos catch the light just right!

INSTRUCTIONS

PATTERN_1

With Color A, CO 28 sts.

Row 1 (WS): P4; (yo, p2tog) to end—28 sts.

Row 2 (RS): Knit to last 4 sts, p4.

Row 3: P4; (k1, p5) across.

Row 4: (K5, p1) across, ending p4.

Row 5: P4; (k1, p5) across.

Row 6: (K5, p1) across, ending p4.

Row 7: P1; (yo, p2tog, p4) across, ending yo, p2tog, p1.

Row 8: Knit to last st, p1.

Row 9: P1; (k1, p5) across, ending p3.

Row 10: K8; (k5, p1) across, ending k5, p2.

Row 11: P1; (k1, p5) across, ending k1, p8.

Row 12: K8, p1; (k5, p1) across, ending k5, p2.

Repeat Pattern 1 seven more times.

PATTERN_2

Note: Color B should always be two strands held together. When changing yarns, bring a new strand from under the previous strand for a "twist" to prevent holes.

Row 1 (RS): With Color A, p4, with Color B, p2, (yo, k2tog) 4 times, k2, yo, k3, sl 1, k1, psso, yo, p2, join another strand of Color A and p5.

Row 2 (and all even rows): With Color A, k5, with Color B knit all knit sts, and purl all purl sts (yarn overs should be worked as purls) to last 4 sts, with Color A, k4.

Row 3: With Color A, p4, with Color B, p2, yo, k2tog, (k3tog) twice, yo, k1, yo, k2, (sl 1, k1, psso, yo) twice, p2, with Color A, p5.

Row 5: With Color A, p4, with Color B, p2, yo, k4tog, yo, k3, yo, k2, (sl 1, k1, psso, yo) twice, p2, with Color A, p5—26 sts.

Row 7: With Color A, p4, with Color B, p2, yo, k2tog, yo, k1, yo, k2, sl 1, k1, psso, yo, k2, (sl 1, k1, psso, yo) twice, p2, with Color A, p5—28 sts.

Row 9: With Color A, p4, with Color B, p2, yo, k2tog, yo, k3, yo, k2, (sl 1, k1, psso) twice (sl 1, k1, psso, yo) twice, p2, with Color A, p5—28 sts.

Row 11: With Color A, p4, with Color B, p2, (yo, k2tog) twice, k2, yo, k1, yo (sl 1, k2tog, psso) twice, sl 1, k1, psso, yo, p2, with Color A, p5—26 sts.

Row 13: With Color A, p4, with Color B, p2, (yo, k2tog) twice, k2, yo, k3, yo, sl 1, k3tog, psso, yo, p2, with Color A, p5—26 sts.

Row 15: With Color A, p4, with Color B, p2, (yo, k2tog) twice, k2, yo, sl 1, k1, psso, k2, yo, k1, yo sl 1, k1, psso, yo, p2, with Color A, p5—28 sts.

Row 16: Repeat Row 2.

Repeat Pattern 1 twenty more times.

Work Pattern 2 once more.

Work Pattern 1 an additional eight times.

BO.

Weave in all ends.

: SKILL LEVEL

Intermediate

: SIZE

Adult women's medium (men's small, men's medium)

: FINISHED MEASUREMENT

11 (12, 14)" [28 (30, 36) cm] circumference at cuff

: MATERIALS

Lion Brand Hometown USA (100% acrylic; 5 oz/140 g; 81 yd/7 m): 1 skein in #099 Los Angeles Tan (Color A)

Patons Divine (76.5% acrylic/10.5% wool/10.5% mohair/2.5% polyester; 3.5 oz/ 100 g; 142 yd/129 m), or any other furry yarn you have lying around: 1 skein in #06013 Deep Earth (Color B)

Four size 11 (8 mm) double-pointed needles

Size H crochet hook

Stitch marker

: GAUGE

8 stitches and 14 rows = 4" (10 cm) in Stockinette stitch on size 11 (8 mm) needles

HOBBIT FEET SLIPPERS

: DESIGNED BY TONI CARR

Hobbits are known for having big, hairy feet that protect them from the elements. They don't even need shoes! Since, perhaps luckily, we don't have hobbit feet, these hobbit feet house slippers will keep your toes nice and toasty with the bonus of not having to shave!

When knit in the round, this pattern knits up very, very fast! The hair is added in later and is a great stash buster for leftover fun fur yarn or any sort of darker mohair. It's also super easy to customize this pattern for the tiniest hobbit to the largest troll in your life.

INSTRUCTIONS

With Color A, CO 24 (28, 32) sts, pm, join in the round.

Rnds 1–7 (8, 10): (K1, p1) around.

Divide for heel.

K6, (9, 11), sl 8 (9, 10) sts from previous needle onto same needle, for heel, hold remaining sts on other needles for instep.

You should have 14 (18, 21) sts on needle to work heel and 10 (10, 11) held in reserve for instep.

HEEL

Row 1: With WS facing, p1, k1, p2tog, p6 (10, 13), p2tog, k1, p1—12 (16, 19) sts.

Row 2: K1, (k1, sl 1) to last st, knit final st.

Row 3: K1, purl to last st, k1.

Repeat Rows 2 and 3 for 3 (4, 6) more times.

Next row: K5 (7, 9), k2tog, k5 (7, 8)—11 (15, 18) sts.

SHAPE HEEL

Row 1: P8 (12, 15), p2tog, p1—10 (14, 17) sts.

Row 2: K7 (11, 14), sl 1, k1, psso, k1—9 (13, 16) sts.

Row 3: P6 (10, 13), p2tog, p1—8 (12, 15) sts.

Row 4: K5 (9, 12), sl 1, k1, psso, k1—7 (11, 14) sts.

Row 5: P4 (8, 11), p2tog, p1—6 (10, 13) sts.

Row 6: K4 (7, 10), k2tog, k0 (1, 1)—5 (9, 12) sts.

With RS facing, pick up and k10 (11,13) sts along the side of heel.

Knit across 10 (10, 11) sts for instep.

Pick up and k10 (11, 13) sts along the side of heel—35 (41, 49) sts.

Divide sts as follows:

Needle 1: 10 (12, 14) sts.

Needle 2: 15 (17, 21) instep sts.

Needle 3: 10 (12, 14) sts.

DECREASE ROWS

Row 1:

Needle 1: Knit to last 3 sts, k2tog, k1.

Needle 2: Knit.

Needle 3: K1, sl 1, k1, psso, knit to end.

Row 2: Knit.

Repeat Rows 1 and 2 for 6 (7, 8) more times—23 (27, 33) sts.

Measure your foot.

Knit around to 1" (3 cm) before total foot length.

Note: If you want the slippers to be big hobbit-feet sized, knit to full foot length before shaping toes.

SHAPE TOES

Row 1:

Needle 1: Knit to last 3 sts, k2tog, k1—3 (4, 5) sts.

Needle 2: K1 (2, 3), sl 1, k1, psso, (k1, k2tog) three times, k1, k2tog, k0 (1, 2)—10 (12, 16) sts.

Needle 3: K1, sl 1, k1, psso, k1 (2, 3)—3 (4, 5) sts.

Knit one round on 16 (20, 26) sts.

MEN'S SIZES ONLY

Next Row:

Needle 1: K2tog, k1.

Needle 2: K1, sl 1, k1, psso, knit to last 3 sts, k2tog, k1.

Needle 3: K1, sl 1, k1, psso.

ALL SIZES

Divide sts evenly onto two needles.

Work Kitchener st to close toe opening.

Weave in loose ends on WS.

FINISHING

With Color B, cut twelve pieces of 2" fringe. Using size H crochet hook, pull through top of foot and on toes. Tie in knot to secure. (This part doesn't need to be perfect. Hobbits' foot hair doesn't grow in straight lines.) Trim pieces of fringe to uneven lengths, then fluff with hairbrush.

Weave in all ends.

: SKILL LEVEL

Intermediate

: FINISHED MEASUREMENTS

68" (173 cm) long and 19" (48 cm) wide after blocking

: MATERIALS

Knit Picks Comfy Fingering (75% cotton, 25% acrylic; 50 g/ 218 yd): 4 skeins in #24823 Lilac Mist

Thirteen beads of your choice, to adorn the fringe

Size 5 (3.75 mm) 24" (61 cm) circular needle, or four double-pointed needles

Five stitch markers (see Special Instructions)

Tapestry needle

: GAUGE

26 stitches and 28 rows = 4" (10 cm) in Stockinette stitch on size 5 (3.75 mm) needles, though gauge is not critical with this pattern.

SUMMER QUEEN SHAWL

: DESIGNED BY RILANA RILEY-MUNSON

This lace shawl is inspired by the urban fantasy novel *Wicked Lovely* by Melissa Marr. Aislinn is a teenager who can see fairies walking among the world. Out of fear for her life, she struggles to keep it a secret. Despite her best efforts to avoid the fae, she finds herself entering their world in an effort to save humans and fairies alike from an endless winter.

Inspired by the idea of Aislinn facing down Winter Queen and her court, this shawl features a repeating panel of leaves through-out the length of the shawl.

SPECIAL INSTRUCTIONS

The stitch markers are optional. To keep track of stitches, it may be helpful to mark each pattern repeat.

sl1-k2tog-psso: Slip 1 stitch purl-wise, knit 2 stitches together, pass the slipped stitch over the previous stitch.

PATTERN_STITCH

Row 1 (and all WS rows): Purl to end.

Row 2 (RS): P2; *k9, yo, k1, yo, k3, sl1-k2tog-psso, p2; repeat * to end.

Row 4: P2; *k10, yo, k1, yo, k2, sl1-k2tog-psso, p2; repeat * to end.

Row 6: P2; *k3tog, k4, yo, k1, yo, k3, (yo, k1) twice, sl1-k2tog-psso, p2; repeat * to end.

Row 8: P2; *k3tog, k3, yo, k1, yo, k9, p2; repeat * to end.

Row 10: P2; *k3tog, k2, yo, k1, yo, k10, p2; repeat * to end.

Row 12: P2; *k3tog, (k1, yo) twice, k3, yo, k1, yo, k4, sl1-k2tog-psso, p2; repeat * to end.

INSTRUCTIONS

TO_MAKE_THE_SHAWL

CO 110 sts.

Knit one row.

Begin with Row 2 of Pattern Stitch. Continue with Pattern Stitch, ending after Row 12.

Continue to work the Pattern Stitch Rows 1–12 until approximately 56" (142 cm), or desired length. Be sure to end on Row 12.

Knit one row.

BO all sts k-wise.

FINISHING

Block (page 122) to the measurements mentioned under Finished Measurements. When the shawl is completely dry, you can add the beads and fringe.

BEADS AND FRINGE

Cut twenty-six (18"/46 cm) pieces of yarn for the fringe, and two pieces of yarn for each point on the ends of the shawl. For one point on the shawl, thread two pieces of yarn through a tapestry needle and pull halfway through the point. Keeping the two threads on the needle, thread through one bead. Remove the thread from the needle and thread the opposite ends of the two pieces of yarn onto the needle. Then thread this end through the bead, forming a loop. Remove the needle and pull the bead to the top and tie a knot to hold the bead at the top. Repeat this for all points on the bottom of the shawl. You will do this a total of thirteen times. One end of the shawl has six points and the other has seven points.

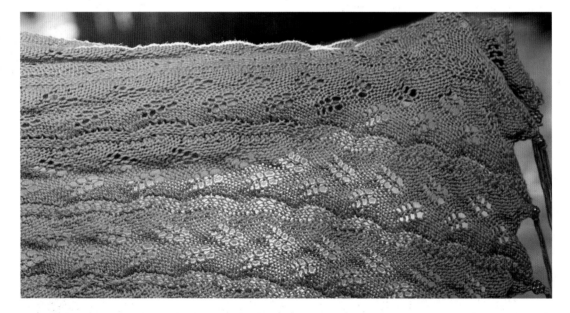

: SKILL LEVEL

Advanced

: SIZE

One size

: FINISHED MEASUREMENTS

8" (20 cm) circumference and 10¾" (27 cm) long from lace edge to top of middle finger

: MATERIALS

Araucania Nature Wool (100% wool; 100 g/ 240 yd/220 m): 1 skein in #R021 Maroon

Four size 4 (3.5 mm) double-pointed needles

Stitch holders

Four stitch markers

Tapestry needle

: GAUGE

28 stitches and 33 rows = 4" (10 cm) in 1 x 1 rib stitch on size 4 (3.55 mm) needles

DRAGON RIDER GLOVES

: DESIGNED BY TONI CARR

Naomi Novik's Temeraire series retells the story of the Napoleonic era but has dragons who work with both French and British military forces. Novik describes each dragon richly and beautifully, and her dragons' scales inspired these gloves. The lace pattern is fairly simple to do. Working seamlessly in the round, you add the fingers and thumb at the end. Start these the second you receive your dragon egg and see how many pairs you can make before it hatches!

PATTERN_STITCH

Row 1: K1; *(yo, ssk) twice, k1, (k2tog, yo) twice, k1; repeat from *.

Row 2: K2; *yo, ssk, yo, sl 2 sts as one k-wise, k1, p2sso, yo, k2tog, yo, k3, repeat from * to last 9 sts, yo, ssk, yo, sl 2 sts as one k-wise, k1, p2sso, yo, k2tog, yo, k2.

INSTRUCTIONS

With DPNs, CO 45 sts; divide evenly over three needles.

Join, pm, (k1, p1) for 14 sts, pm, k31.

Rnd 1: (K1, p1) rib over 14 sts, sm, k1; *(yo, ssk) twice, k1, (k2tog, yo) twice, k1. Repeat from * to second marker.

Rnd 2: (K1, p1) over 14 sts, sm, knit to marker.

Rnd 3: (K1, p1) over 14 sts, sm, k2; *yo, ssk, yo, sl 2 sts as one, k-wise, k1, p2sso, yo, k2tog, yo, k3, repeat from * to last 9 sts; yo, ssk, yo, sl 2 sts as one k-wise, k1, p2sso, yo, k2tog, yo, k2 sts between markers, k2.

Rnd 4: (K1, p1) over 14 sts, sm, knit to marker.

Repeat Rnds 1–4 for 4" (10 cm), then work Rnds 1–3 again before beginning thumb gusset.

LEFT_HAND

Rnd 1: Rib 14, sm, pm (a different colored marker is helpful), M1, k1, M1, pm, knit to end—3 thumb sts.

Rnd 2: Rib 14, knit thumb sts, work Row 1 of Pattern Stitch.

Rnd 3: Rib 14, sm, M1, sm, M1, k3, M1, sm, knit to end—6 thumb sts.

Rnd 4: Rib 14, sm, knit to marker, sm, knit to marker, sm, work Row 2 of Pattern Stitch.

Rnd 5: Rib 14, sm, k1, sm, M1, k5, M1, sm, knit to end—8 thumb sts.

Rnd 6: Repeat Rnd 2.

Rnd 7: Rib 14, sm, M1, k1, sm, M1, knit to marker, M1, sm, knit to end—11 thumb sts.

Rnd 8: Repeat Rnd 4.

Rnd 9: Rib 14, sm, k2, sm, knit to marker, sm, knit to end.

Rnd 10: Repeat Rnd 2.

Rnd 11: Rib 14, sm, k2, sm, knit to marker, sm, knit to end.

RIGHT_HAND

Rnd 1: Rib 14, knit to last 2 sts, pm (a different colored marker is helpful), M1, k1, M1, pm—3 thumb sts.

Rnd 2: Rib 14, knit thumb sts, work Row 1 of Pattern Stitch.

Rnd 3: Rib 14, knit to marker, sm, M1, k1, M1, knit to marker, M1, sm—6 thumb sts.

Rnd 4: Rib 14, sm, work Row 2 of Pattern Stitch, sm, knit to marker, sm.

Rnd 5: Rib 14, knit to marker sm, k1, M1, knit to marker, M1, sm—8 thumb sts.

Rnd 6: Repeat Rnd 2.

Rnd 7: Rib 14, knit to marker, sm, M1, k1, M1, knit to marker, M1, sm—11 thumb sts.

Rnd 8: Repeat Rnd 4.

Rnd 9: Rib 14, knit to marker, sm, knit to marker, sm.

Rnd 10: Repeat Rnd 2.

Rnd 11: Rib 14, knit to marker, sm, knit to marker, sm.

FOR_BOTH_HANDS

Rnd 12: Work established rib, sm, slip all thumb sts to holder, removing markers, working Row 2 of Pattern Stitch.

Rnd 13: Work established rib, knit to end.

Rnd 14: Work established rib, Row 1 of Pattern Stitch.

Rnd 15: Work established rib, knit to end.

Rnd 16: Work established rib, Row 2 of Pattern Stitch.

Rnds 17–30: Repeat Rnds 13–16.

Rnds 31–32: Knit all sts.

DIVIDE_STS_FOR_FINGER_GUSSETS

Index finger: Divide 12 sts evenly among three needles.

Join, pm, and knit ten rnds.

BO.

Middle finger: Divide 14 sts among three needles.

Pm and join, picking up 2 sts in between index and middle fingers.

Knit twelve rnds.

BO.

Ring finger: Divide 11 sts among three needles.

Pm and join, picking up 2 sts between ring and middle fingers.

Knit twelve rnds.

BO.

Pinky finger: Divide 7 sts among three needles.

Pm and join, picking up 2 sts between ring and pinky fingers.

Knit ten rnds.

Note: The best way to do this is to take your first 12 sts for your index finger and place the remaining sts on stitch holders.

THUMB

Slip sts from st holder to DPN, picking up 3 sts from glove edge, pm, and join.

Knit eight rnds.

BO.

FINISHING

Weave in all ends. Block lightly to even out the lace stitch and bottom edge. Wear the gloves to keep the cold at bay on high-altitude rides.

: SKILL LEVEL

Advanced

: SIZE

Small (medium, large, extra large)

: FINISHED MEASUREMENT

10 (11, 12, 13)" [25 (28, 30, 33) cm] upper arm circumference

: MATERIALS

Knit Picks Bare Shadow Lace Yarn (100% Merino wool; 100g/880 yd): 1 (1, 1, 2) hanks in Bare

Aurora Borealis glass seed beads 5 oz/ 140 g (5.7 oz/160 g, 6.4 oz/180 g, 7.1 oz/ 200 g) 6/0

Size 6 (4 mm) double-pointed needles

Four size 8 (5 mm) double-pointed needles

No. 14 (0.5 mm) beading crochet hook

Size G (4 mm) crochet hook

Stitch markers

Tapestry needle

: GAUGE

23 stitches and 25 rows = 4" (10 cm) in Stockinette stitch on size 6 (4 mm) needles

LIGHT OF EÄRENDIL SHRUG

: DESIGNED BY ASHLEY FAY

The Light of Eärendil shrug is inspired by the beautiful elf Galadriel from *The Lord of the Rings*. She gave the Light of Eärendil to Sam to use as a light in dark places. The leaf pattern, star stitch, and beading represent Galadriel.

SPECIAL INSTRUCTIONS

Twist Stitch (T): Twist stitch by knitting through the back loop.

Place Bead (B): Place bead over crochet hook, use hook to lift specified stitch off of the left needle and slide the bead over the stitch, place stitch back on left needle and knit as you normally would.

Star Stitch (SS): K3tog but don't drop these 3 stitches off the left needle, yo right needle and knit same 3 stitches together and now drop the 3 stitches off of the left needle.

SS Increase (SSinc): K1 without dropping stitch off left needle, yo, k1 in same stitch and drop stitch off left needle.

Make Two (M2): Insert left needle from front to back into vertical bar before next st. Knit in back and front of this loop.

★★★ INSTRUCTIONS

FIRST_SLEEVE

Using smaller needles, CO 48 (56, 60, 68) sts using scrap yarn and a provisional cast on. PO (4, 6, 10), pm, and begin Leaf Chart, work Row 1 across next 24 sts, pm and repeat Row 1 across next 24 sts, pm, p0 (4, 6, 10) sts; do not join.

Continue in this manner, working all rows of the Leaf Chart until piece measures 7½ (8, 8½, 9)" [19 (20, 22, 23) cm]. Make note of ending row.

Pm and join to work in the round. Continue working established chart, noting that [O] is now purl on both RS and WS rnds. Work even to 28 (28½, 29, 29½)" [71 (72, 74, 75) cm] from beg.

Change to larger needles.

(M1, k12) four times, ending k0 (8, 12, 20) sts—52 (60, 64, 72) remaining sts.

Begin Star Pattern for Cuff.

STAR PATTERN FOR CUFF

Rnd 1 (RS): *K1, SS (see note); repeat from * to end of rnd.

Rnd 2: K1, B, *k3, B; repeat from * to last 2 sts, k2.

Rnd 3: *SS, k1; repeat from * to end of rnd.

Rnd 4: B; *K3, B; repeat from * to last 3 sts, k3.

Rnd 5: (K1, SS) 3 (3, 4, 4) times total, M2. (K1, SS) 3 (4, 4, 4) times total, M2. (K1, SS) 3 (4, 4, 5) times total, M2. (K1, SS) 4 (4, 4, 5) times total, M2—60 (68, 72, 86) sts.

Rnd 6: Knit all stitches while placing a bead on the first stitch of each SS.

Rnd 7: (SS, k1) 3 (3, 4, 4) times total, SSinc, k1. (SS, k1) 3 (4, 4, 4) times total, SSinc, k1.

(SS, k1) 3 (4, 4, 5) times total, SSinc, k1. (SS, k1) 4 (4, 4, 5) times total, SSinc, k1—68 (76, 80, 88) sts.

Rnd 8: Repeat Rnd 6.

Rnds 9–12: Repeat Rnds 1–4.

Rnd 13: (K1, SS) 4 (4, 5, 5) times total, M2. (K1, SS) 4 (5, 5, 5) times total, M2. (K1, SS) 4 (5, 5, 6) times, M2. (K1, SS) 5 (5, 5, 6) times total, M2—76 (84, 88, 96) sts.

Rnd 14: Knit all stitches while placing a bead on the first stitch of each SS.

Rnd 15: (SS, k1) 4 (4, 5, 5) times total, SSinc, k1. (SS, k1) 4 (5, 5, 5) times total, SSinc, k1. (SS, k1) 4 (5, 5, 6) times total, SSinc, k1. (SS, k1) 5 (5, 5, 6) times total, SSinc, k1—84 (92, 96, 104) sts.

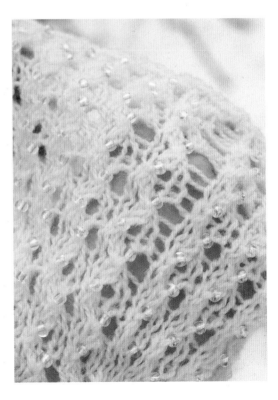

Rnd 16: Repeat Rnd 14.

Repeat Rnds 1–4 until piece measures 36 [36½, 37, 37½]" [91 (93, 94, 95) cm].

BO.

Remove provisional cast on and place stitches on smaller needles. Make second sleeve as for first, using your now live stitches from your provisional cast on edge.

PICOT EDGING

With RS facing and crochet hook, beginning at an armpit corner, where you joined to work in the rnd, work 3 sc, ch 4, sc in same space—picot made. Repeat until your picot border is complete.

★ LEAF CHART

Legend:

(blank)	For St st, knit on right side, purl on wrong side for rows. For rounds, knit each round.
•	For reverse St st, purl on right side, knit on wrong side for rows. For rounds, purl on right side and wrong side.
T	Twist stitch, see note
B	Place bead, see note
O	Yarn over
/	K2tog
\	SSK
⅄	Slip 1, k2tog, PSSO

Row/Rnd 1 (RS)

SKILL LEVEL

Intermediate

FINISHED MEASUREMENT

13 (14, 15)" [33 (36, 38) cm] circumference

MATERIALS

Bernat Softee Chunky (100% acrylic; 3.5 oz/ 100 g; 180 yd/164 m): 1 skein each in #39222 Fern (Color A) and #39008 Natural (Color B)

Size 8 (5 mm) 16" (41 cm) circular needle

Four size 8 (5 mm) double-pointed needles

Stitch markers

Tapestry needle

GAUGE

16 stitches and 20 rows = 4" (10 cm) in Stockinette stitch on size 8 (5 mm) needles

BABY ELF BEANIE

: DESIGNED BY TONI CARR

You are never too young for your first fantasy costume at the convention! Whip up this cute hat in hours and give it to your favorite little elf! The beanie is knit in the round with elf ears picked up and worked in Stockinette stitch at the end.

This hat is also easy to modify for other costume ideas. Knit it all in red for a little devil! Or knit the base in brown and the ears in gold for a baby Viking helmet!

INSTRUCTIONS

HAT

With Color A, CO 50 (60, 70) sts, pm, and join in the round.

Knit every rnd 16 (18, 20) times for St st.

CROWN SHAPING (CHANGE TO DPNS WHEN NEEDED)

Rnd 1: (K8, k2tog) around—45 (54, 63) sts.

Rnd 2: Knit.

Rnd 3: Knit.

Rnd 4: (K7, k2tog) around—40 (48, 56) sts.

Rnd 5: Knit.

Rnd 6: Knit.

Rnd 7: Knit.

Rnd 8: (K6, k2tog) around—35 (42, 49) sts.

Rnd 9: Knit.

Rnd 10: Knit.

Rnd 11: (K5, k2tog) around—30 (36, 42) sts.

Rnd 12: Knit.

Rnd 13: (K4, k2tog) around—25 (30, 35) sts.

Rnd 14: Knit.

Rnd 15: (K3, k2tog) around—20 (24, 28) sts.

Rnd 16: Knit.

Rnd 17: K2tog around—10 (12, 14) sts.

Cut yarn and pull tail through remaining sts.

EARS

Measure 1½ (1½, 2)" [4 (4, 6) cm] from bottom of hat on each side. *(Note: Bottom of hat = bottom of roll, not CO edge.)* With Color B, pick up and k8 (8, 10) sts up side of hat.

LEFT EAR
for small

Purl one row.

For medium and large

Beginning with a purl row, work St st for 5 (5, 7) rows.

For all sizes

Row 1 (RS): K2tog, knit to end—7 (7, 9) sts.

Row 2: Purl.

Row 3: K2tog, knit to end—6 (6, 8) sts.

Row 4: Purl.

Row 5: K2tog twice, knit to end—4 (4, 6) sts.

Row 6: Purl.

Row 7: K2tog, knit to end—3 (3, 5) sts.

Row 8: Purl.

Row 9: K2tog, knit to end—2 (2, 4) sts.

For small and medium

P2tog.

For large

Next Row: Purl.

Next Row: K2tog twice.

Next Row: P2tog.

All sizes

BO. Cut the tail and pull it through the remaining stitch.

Repeat for Right Ear.

FINISHING

With a tapestry needle and Color B, stitch the points of each ear to each side of the hat. For a pointier elf ear, leave the ear points unattached.

: SKILL LEVEL

Intermediate

: FINISHED MEASUREMENTS

38" (96½ cm) circumference and 17" (14 cm) tall before felting

23½" (60 cm) circumference and 7¾" (20 cm) tall after felting (see Note)

: MATERIALS

Knit Picks Wool of the Andes (100% Peruvian highland wool; 50 g/ 110 yd): 3 skeins in #23439 Grass

Size 8 (5 mm) 16" (40 cm) circular needle

Four size 8 (5 mm) double-pointed needles

Stitch marker

: GAUGE

Before felting, 19 stitches and 25 rows = 4" (10 cm) in Stockinette stitch on size 8 (5 mm) needles

MR. NANCY'S HAT

: DESIGNED BY TONI CARR

Neil Gaiman is easily one of my favorite writers. His books never fail to inspire me. I often found myself reading his comic books and (to the delight of my teachers) researching Greek history. Other times I would be so inspired by a character that (to the dismay of my mother) I would get a tattoo. With *Anansi Boys*, however, I found myself inspired to knit!

Mr. Nancy is described as wearing a green fedora, a bold look that requires a certain amount of confidence to carry off. I decided to create my own version of this awesome green hat. Knit in the round and then felted and shaped when wet, this hat looks complicated but even a newer knitter could take on this project!

INSTRUCTIONS

Using the circular needle, CO 180 sts, pm, and join for working in the round.

Knit around for 6" (15 cm).

Next rnd: (K10, k2tog) around—165 sts.

Knit two rnds.

Next rnd: (K8, k2tog) to last 5 sts, k5—149 sts.

Knit two rnds.

Next rnd: (K6, k2tog) to last 5 sts, k5—131 sts.

Knit around until hat measures 14" (36 cm) total.

CROWN SHAPING
(CHANGE TO DPNS AS NECESSARY)

Next rnd: (K6, k2tog) to last 3 sts, k3—115 sts.

Knit two rnds.

Next rnd: (K4, k2tog) to last st, k1—96 sts.

Knit two rnds.

Next rnd: (K2, k2tog) around—72 sts.

Knit two rnds.

Next rnd: (K1, k2tog) around—48 sts.

Knit two rnds.

Next rnd: K2tog around until 6 sts remain.

Cut yarn, thread through remaining stitches, and pull closed.

FINISHING

Weave in all ends.

Felt the hat (page 125). Once the hat is felted and shrunk to size, pinch the top to form the front and sides of the fedora and gently pull out the brim. Next, stuff the hat with paper or towels to hold its shape while drying.

Note: The great thing about this hat is that you can make it fit your head. Measure your head, then take a piece of cardboard and cut it into a long strip about 3" wide and the length of the circumference of your head. While blocking (or drying your hat), place the strip of cardboard inside the hat. This will help your hat keep the shape and not shrink smaller than your head size.

QUESTION:

If you noticed that you can see fairies, what should your reaction be?

A. Walk up and say, "Hi!" Fae are friendly!

B. Take off running as fast as you can!

C. Act like you can't see them at all, no matter what they do to attract your attention.

Answer: C. If you're seeing fae, you're living in Melissa Marr's *Wicked Lovely* world! If a fairy realizes that you can see them, they'll take your eyes!

: SKILL LEVEL

Intermediate

: SIZE

Men's size small
(medium, large)

: FINISHED MEASUREMENTS

Small = 6" (15 cm)
circumference at wrist
and about 7¾" (20 cm)
long

Medium = 7" (18 cm)
circumference at wrist
and about 8" (20 cm)
long

Large = 8" (20 cm)
circumference at wrist
and about 9" (23 cm)
long

: MATERIALS

Knit Picks Swish DK
(100% superwash Merino
wool; 50 g/123 yd):
2 skeins in #24634
Semolina

Five size 4 (3.5 mm)
double-pointed needles

Three stitch holders

Stitch markers

: GAUGE

29 stitches and 31
rows = 4" (10 cm) in
Stockinette stitch on
size 4 (3.5 mm) needles

MR. NANCY'S GLOVES

: DESIGNED BY TONI CARR

While Neil Gaiman's *Anansi Boys* lets us get
to know Mr. Nancy and family, it's actually his
book *American Gods* where we first meet Mr.
Nancy. Gaiman describes him as wearing a
"bright checked suit and canary yellow gloves."
While he only plays a brief role in *American
Gods*, his charm and sense of humor make him
a fast favorite character.

As a tribute to Mr. Nancy, knit up your own
canary yellow gloves! They are quick to knit and
fun to wear!

INSTRUCTIONS [MAKE 2]

CO 52 (56, 60) sts and divide evenly onto four needles.

PM and join.

Work (k1, p1) rib for 10 (12, 12) rows.

Beginning with a knit row, work six St st rows.

First rnd (RS): K2, pm, knit around.

*Note: It's a good idea to use a different colored marker for
the Thumb Gusset.*

THUMB GUSSET

Rnd 1: Knit to 1 st before marker, M1, k1, sm, k1, M1, knit
to end—54 (58, 62) sts.

Rnds 2–4: Knit.

Repeat last four rnds 3 (4, 4) times more—60 (66, 70) sts.

Next rnd: Sl 6 (7, 7) sts before thumb gusset marker and place on holder, knit next 6 (7, 7) sts and place on holder, knit remaining sts—48 (52, 56) sts.

Knit around for 1¾ (2 2½)" [4 (5, 6) cm].

Note: As you knit the fingers for the gloves, it is a great idea to try them on to ensure a perfect fit!

FINGERS

INDEX FINGER

Sl 6 (8, 8) before marker and 6 (8, 8) sts after marker to working needles.

*Divide remaining 36 (36, 40) sts evenly onto two stitch holders. *

Knit around for 2¾ (3, 3)" [7 (8, 8) cm].

(K2tog) around to last 2 sts. Cut tail and pull through.

MIDDLE FINGER

Sl 6 (8, 10) from each stitch holder (see * to * above) onto working needles. Pick up and k2 sts between index finger and middle finger—24 (20, 20) sts remain on holders.

Knit around on 14 (18, 22) sts for 3 (3½, 3½)" [8 (9, 9) cm].

(K2tog) around to last 2 sts.

Cut tail and pull through.

RING FINGER

Sl 8 (7, 7) sts from each holder onto working needles. Pick up and k2 sts between middle and ring fingers—8 (6, 6) sts remain on holder.

Knit around on 14 (16, 20) sts for 2¾ (3, 3)" [7 (8, 8) cm].

(K2tog) around to last 2 sts.

Cut tail and pull through.

PINKY FINGER

Slip remaining sts from each holder to working needles. Pick up and k2 sts between ring and pinky fingers—8 (6, 6) sts.

Knit around for 2 (2½, 2½)" [5 (6, 6) cm].

(K2tog) around to last 2 sts.

Cut tail and pull through.

THUMB

Sl 12 (14, 14) sts from first holder onto working needles. Pick up and k4 (6, 8) sts. Knit around on 16 (20, 22) sts for 2½ (3, 3)" [6 (8, 8) cm].

(K2tog) around to last 2 sts. Cut tail and pull through.

Weave in all remaining ends and wear with flair, especially while going to karaoke nights!

SKILL LEVEL

Intermediate

FINISHED MEASUREMENTS

14" (36 cm) wide and 13" (33 cm) long

MATERIALS

Cushendale Worsted Weight Yarn (100% wool; 4 oz/100 g, 164 yd/227 m): 1 skein in Old Purple [Note: This yarn is produced in Ireland. Any worsted weight tweedy yarn should work, such as Knit Picks City Tweed (55% Merino wool, 25% superfine alpaca, 20% Donegal tweed; 50 g/123 yd)]

Seven chunky silver beads (I used Darice Jewelry Designer BV Antique Silver)

Thirty-two round purple beads (I used Darice Jewelry Designer 8mm Resin Round Beads in Purple)

Size 8 (5 mm) 16" (41 cm) circular needle

Four size 8 (5 mm) double-pointed needles

Stitch marker

Size H-8 (5 mm) crochet hook

GAUGE

20 stitches and 24 rows = 4" (10cm) in Stockinette stitch on size 8 (5 mm) needles

SECRET BEADED BAG

DESIGNED BY TONI CARR

One of the most popular themes in both science fiction and fantasy is that an object can be bigger on the inside than it is on the outside. In *Harry Potter and the Deathly Hallows*, for instance, Hermione Granger charms a small beaded purse to fit months' worth of books and supplies while the young wizards are trying to discover a way to defeat the evil wizard Voldemort.

While you may not be able to fit fifty textbooks, a tent, and multiple changes of clothes in this version, it's still a lovely alternative to a clunky purse for a night out. Stash your ID, cell phone, and your copy of *Fantastic Beasts and Where to Find Them* inside!!

SPECIAL INSTRUCTIONS

Sl1b: Slip one bead. Bring yarn to front of work as if to purl, slip next stitch, slip bead close to last stitch worked, move yarn to back, knit next stitch. The bead will be in front of the slipped stitch. Before casting on, string all the beads onto your yarn.

INSTRUCTIONS

Thread (1 silver bead, 5 purple beads) onto your yarn five times, then 1 silver and 2 purple.

CO 70 sts, pm, and join in the round.

Rnd 1: (K1, yo, k2tog) around, ending k1.

Rnd 2: Knit.

Rnd 3: Knit.

Rnd 4: Knit.

Rnd 5: Repeat Rnd 1.

Rnd 6: (K2, sl1b) around, ending k1—23 beads added.

Rnds 7–11: Knit.

Rnd 12: Repeat Rnd 1.

Rnd 13: (K6, sl1b) around—10 beads added.

Rnds 14–17: Knit.

Rnd 18 (Drawstring Round): (K2, yo, k2tog) to last 2 sts, k2.

Knit around for 8" (20 cm) from Drawstring Round.

DECREASE ROUNDS

(Switch to double-pointed needles when necessary.)

Rnd 1: (K8, k2tog) around—63 sts.

Rnd 2: Knit.

Rnd 3: (K6, k2tog) to last 7 sts, k5, k2tog—55 sts.

Rnd 4: Knit.

Rnd 5: (K4, k2tog) to last st, k1—46 sts.

Rnd 6: Knit.

Rnd 7: (K2, k2tog) to last 2 sts, k2—35 sts.

Rnd 8: Knit.

(K2tog) around to last 5 sts.

Cut yarn, leaving an 8" (20 cm) tail, and pull tail through remaining sts to close base of bag.

DRAWSTRING

Thread 1 silver bead, 1 purple bead, 1 silver bead, and 1 purple bead onto yarn. With crochet hook, ch 2, slide one bead, ch 2, slide one bead, ch 4, slide one bead, ch 4, slide one bead. Continue working chain st for a total of 24" (61 cm).

Are you having trouble threading your beads? Try threading a sewing needle with a little bit of thread, then tie that thread to the end of your yarn. Thread the needle through your beads and pull the yarn through after!

FINISHING

Thread the drawstring through the holes created on the Drawstring Row. Fill the bag with as much stuff as it can hold (which is more than what it looks like) and pull tight!

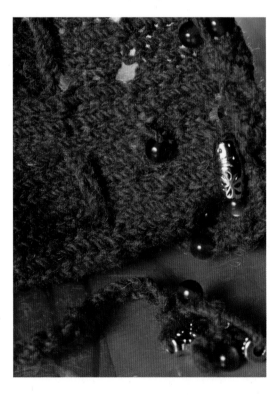

SECTION_2
SCIENCE FICTION

- **SKILL LEVEL**

  Intermediate

- **SIZE**

  One size

- **FINISHED MEASUREMENTS**

  9¾" (25 cm) long and 9"
  (23 cm) wide

- **MATERIALS**

  Knit Picks Swish DK
  (100% superwash Merino
  wool; 50 g/123 yd): 1
  skein each in #24057
  Moss (Color A) and
  #24633 Bark (Color B)

  Twelve ¼"/½ cm buttons

  Size 4 (3.5 mm) straight
  needles

  Stitch markers

  Sewing needle and thread
  in corresponding colors

- **GAUGE**

  20 stitches and 32
  rows = 4" (10 cm) in
  Stockinette stitch on
  size 4 (3.5 mm) needles

HORRIBLE GLOVES

: DESIGNED BY TONI CARR

Dr. Horrible's Sing-Along Blog was one of the most entertaining Internet sensations I have ever seen! A Joss Whedon production, it featured a cast considered the coolest of the cool among the gamer/sci-fi community. Dr. Horrible keeps a video blog where he laments his exclusion from a group of evil villains, vents his frustrations with the "good guy" Captain Hammer, and chronicles Dr. Horrible's attempts to get the beautiful and kind Penny to notice him.

These gloves were created based on what Penny wore on her date with Captain Hammer. Knit flat, they feature a nice stretchy seed stitch at the top and bottom. Buttons make a cute accent on the front. Make these in the muted earth tones featured, or spice them up with bright colors and buttons!

SPECIAL INSTRUCTIONS

Make Two (M2): Insert left needle from front to back into vertical bar before next st. Knit in back and front of this loop.

INSTRUCTIONS

With Color B, CO 48 sts.

Row 1 (RS): (K1, p1) to end.

Row 2: (P1, k1) to end.

Continue in seed stitch for a total of 6 rows from beginning.

STRIPE_PATTERN

Note: Use three separate strands of yarn. When changing color, bring next strand from under previous strand for a twist to prevent holes.

Row (RS) 1: With Color B, (k1, p1) twice, with Color A, knit to last 4 sts, with Color B, (k1, p1) twice.

Row 2: With Color B, p1, BO 2, with Color A, purl to last 4 sts, with Color B, (p1, k1) twice.

Row 3: With Color B, (k1, p1) twice, with Color A, knit to last 2 sts, with Color B, k1, CO 2, p1.

Row 4: With Color B, (p1, k1) twice, with Color A, purl to last 4 sts, with Color B, (p1, k1) twice.

Row 5: With Color B, (k1, p1) twice, with Color A, knit to last 4 sts, with Color B, (k1, p1) twice.

Row 6: With Color B, (p1, k1) twice, with Color A, purl to last 4 sts, with Color B, (p1, k1) twice.

Rows 7–12: With Color B, repeat Rows 1–6.

Work last 12 rows for stripe pattern.

Work stripe pattern a total of four times.

THUMB_GUSSET

Note: For Left Glove, work instructions below with [brackets] indicating instructions for left glove.

Row 1 (RS): With Color B, (k1, p1) twice, with Color A, k16 [for Left Glove, k22 instead], M1, k1, pm, k1, M1, knit to last 4 sts, with Color B (k1, p1) twice—50 sts.

Row 2: With Color B, p1, BO 2, with Color A, purl to last 4 sts, with Color B (p1, k1) twice.

Row 3: With Color B, (k1, p1) twice, with Color A, knit to 1 st before marker, M1, k1, sm, k1, M1, knit to last 4 sts, with Color B (k1, CO2, p1)—52 sts.

Row 4: With Color B, (p1, k1) twice, with Color A, purl to last 4 sts, (p1, k1) twice.

Row 5: With Color B, (k1, p1) twice, with Color A, knit to 1 st before marker, M1, k1, sm, k1, M1, knit to last 4 sts, with Color B (k1, p1) twice—54 sts.

Row 6: With Color B, (p1, k1) twice, with Color A, purl to last 4 sts, (p1, k1) twice.

Row 7: With Color B, (k1, p1) twice, knit to 4 sts before marker, sl 4 sts before marker and 4 sts after marker to holder, cut yarn, and attach

another strand of Color B, knit to last 4 sts, (k1, p1) twice.

Row 8: With Color B, p1, BO 2, purl to thumb gusset, M2, purl to last 4 sts, (p1, k1) twice.

Row 9: With Color B, (k1, p1) twice, knit to last st, CO 2, p1.

Rows 10–12: Continue in established stitch and color patterns.

Repeat 12 rows of stitch and color pattern once again to equal twelve stripes (not including seed st border).

With Color B, work 6 rows of seed st. BO in pattern.

FINISH THUMB

With DPNs and Color A, pick up 6 sts.

Pm, join, and knit around for 6 rows.

BO.

Weave in all ends.

FINISHING

Sew buttons on opposite edge of buttonholes.

QUESTION:

What moniker do *Star Trek* fans prefer?

    A. Trekkies
    B. Trekkers
    C. Storm Troopers

Answer: According to Leonard Nimoy, it's B. Trekkers. And we don't argue with Leonard Nimoy!

: SKILL LEVEL

Easy

: FINISHED MEASUREMENTS

66" (168 cm) long and 7" (18 cm) wide, before pom poms and fringe are attached

: MATERIALS

Knit Picks Swish DK (100% superwash Merino wool; 50g/123 yd): 1 skein each in #24632 Serrano (Color A), #24634 Semolina (Color B), and #24637 Orange (Color C)

Size 8 (5 mm) 29" (74 cm) circular needle

: GAUGE

21 stitches and 20 rows = 4" (10 cm) in garter stitch on size 8 (5 mm) needles

CUNNING SCARF

: DESIGNED BY TONI CARR

Years ago a certain hat took the nerd community by storm! The Jayne Cobb hat, worn by the character Jayne Cobb in the all-too-quickly-canceled *Firefly*, started popping up all over sci-fi conventions. Patterns were posted all over the Internet, and almost every knitting nerd was taking a crack at making one for himself/herself.

Inspired by that hat, knit this Cunning Scarf, to either wear with your hat, or to simply show your love of *Firefly* without messing up your hair!

Knit lengthwise, this is a great scarf for a beginner. A little bit of funky detail in the way of pom-poms and fringe helps it maintain that loving Momma Cobb rustic feel!

INSTRUCTIONS

With Color A, CO 350 sts.

Working back and forth, knit 6 rows.

*With Color B, knit 6 rows.

With Color C, knit 6 rows.*

With Color A, knit 6 rows. Repeat from * to *.

BO.

FINISHING

Make four pom-poms with all three colors (page 127). Attach one on each corner of the scarf.

Use the remaining yarn to make fringe and attach it among the pom-poms (page 125).

HEY! FYI!

Actor Seth Green is the only person to be in both the original *Buffy the Vampire Slayer* movie AND the TV show. Unfortunately, his movie scenes ended up on the cutting room floor!

SKILL LEVEL

Intermediate

SIZE

Small (medium, large)

FINISHED MEASUREMENTS

Circumference: 7¼ (8, 8¾)" [20 (20, 22) cm]

Length to ankle [includes 2" (5 cm) cuff]: 6 (8, 10)" [15 (20, 25) cm]

MATERIALS

Knit Picks Swish DK (100% superwash Merino wool; 50g/123 yd): 1 skein each in #24634 Semolina (Color A), #24632 Serrano (Color B), and #24637 Orange (Color C)

Five size 2 (2.75 mm) double-pointed needles

Four size 3 (3.25 mm) double-pointed needles

Stitch markers

Tapestry needle

GAUGE

6 stitches per 1" (3 cm) on size 3 (3.25 mm) needles in Stockinette stitch

CUNNING SOCKS

: DESIGNED BY LAURA HOHMAN

Like the Cunning Scarf on page 39, these socks are designed to be a play on the Jayne Cobb hat from *Firefly*! Enjoy the envious looks of your peers as you kick off your shoes at the next *Serenity* movie night and show off your "shiny" socks!

SPECIAL INSTRUCTIONS

Color sequence is a repeating A, B, C.

INSTRUCTIONS

CUFF

Using size 2 DPNs, CO 44 (48, 52) sts in Color A.

Arrange on three needles, join, and work in (k2, p2) rib for 2" (5 cm), changing colors every 8 rnds.

BODY

Change to size 3 DPNs and knit every rnd. Change colors every 8 rnds until piece measures 6 (7, 8)" [10 (15, 20) cm] from beginning.

HEEL

Change to the previous row color (not the next one in the sequence).

Turn and p22 (24, 26) sts onto a single needle to work heel.

Leave remaining 22 (24, 26) (instep) sts on two needles. Work heel back and forth as follows:

Row 1: *sl 1 as if to purl, k1; repeat from * to end of row.

Row 2: Sl 1, purl across.

Repeat Rows 1–2 until heel measures 2 (2.5, 3)" [5 (6, 8) cm] or approximately 16 (20, 24) rows, ending with Row 1.

TURN HEEL

Work a series of short rows from center of heel:

Row 1: Sl 1, p12 (12, 14), p2tog, p1, turn.

Row 2: Sl 1, k5, ssk, k1, turn.

Row 3: Sl 1, p6, p2tog, p1, turn.

Row 4: Sl 1, k7, ssk, k1, turn.

Repeat (increasing number of stitches purl or knit each row), until all stitches have been added to row.

There should be 14 (15, 16) stitches remaining.

End heel on a knit row, adding an extra row if necessary.

INSTEP

Using the next color in the sequence from before the heel, pick up and k12 (13, 13) sts on side of heel flap with spare needle

K22 (24, 26) sts (held in reserve for instep) onto second needle.

Pick up and k12 (12, 13) sts on other side of heel flap with third needle and k7 (8, 8) heel sts onto same needle.

PM on first needle and then slip other 7 (7, 8) heel sts onto end of first needle. *Note: Stitch marker notes end of round for color changing.*

There should be a total of 60 (64, 68) sts on three needles at this point.

Needles 1 and 3 should have (19, 20, 21) sts.

Needle 2 should have 22 (24, 26) sts.

DECREASE ROUND

Needle 1: Knit to last 3 sts, ssk, k1.

Needle 2: Knit.

Needle 3: K1, k2tog, knit remaining sts.

Changing colors every 8 rnds, work 1 rnd even and 1 Decrease Round until 44 (48, 52) sts remain.

Needles 1 and 3 should have 11 (12, 13) sts and Needle 2 should have 22 (24, 26) sts.

Knit around on 44 (48, 52) sts until foot measures 2" (5 cm) less than desired length.

TOE SHAPING

Needle 1: Knit to last 3 sts, k2tog, k1.

Needle 2: K1, ssk, knit to last 3 sts, k2tog, k1.

Needle 3: K1, ssk, knit to end.

Repeat one knit round, one Decrease Round until 12 (16, 16) sts remain.

Knit remaining sts from Needle 1 onto Needle 3—6 (8, 8) sts on each needle.

Cut 12" (30 cm) tail of yarn and thread onto tapestry needle.

Hold sock with yarn at right side, tail coming from the rear needle.

Finish toe in Kitchener stitch. Use a tapestry needle to pull the tail through the end of the sock.

Repeat instructions for second sock, either with the same color sequence or, as shown on the model, switch it up a little by starting with Color C and working your stripe sequence from there.

HEY! FYI!

There are places other than science fiction and comic book conventions for nerds to gather together. *WOOtstock*, the slightly disturbing musical show with podcasters Paul and Storm, features lots of hilarity and "squee" worthy moments for fanboys and fangirls!

: SKILL LEVEL

Intermediate

: SIZE

Average adult or child's large

: FINISHED MEASUREMENT

Unstretched hat is 17¼" (44 cm) in circumference

: MATERIALS

Knit Picks Gloss HW (70% Merino wool, 30% silk; 100 g/164 yd): 2 skeins in #24739 Fedora

Size 8 (5 mm) 16" circular needle, or four double-pointed needles

Four size 7 (4.5 mm) double-pointed needles

Tapestry needle

Size G crochet hook, for picking up stitches if necessary

Nine stitch markers

Stuffing for the buns

: GAUGE

24 stitches = 4" (10 cm) in 1x1 rib stitch

SPACE PRINCESS HATS

: DESIGNED BY GENEVIEVE MILLER

Whether you want to look like Princess Leia or just keep your ears warm, this hat is perfect for you! This is really three patterns in one. Once you knit the main part of the hat, there are three hairstyle options to choose from—all the options are based on Leia's hairstyles in the *Star Wars* movies. Use this hat to ward off the chilly weather, or as part of a costume!

INSTRUCTIONS

HAT

With the size 8 circular needle, CO 104 sts.

Join and work around in (k1, p1) rib for 4.5" (11 cm).

DECREASES

Rnd 1: *K2tog, k1, p1, k1, p1, k1, p1, pm; repeat from * for thirteen total times—91 sts.

At this point, start knitting onto DPNs as follows:

Rnd 2: *K2tog, p1, k1, p1, k1, p1, sm; repeat from * two more times on first needle—18 sts.

Start second DPN as follows:

*K2tog, p1, k1, p1, k1, p1, sm; repeat from * two more times on second needle—18 sts.

Start third DPN as follows:

*K2tog, p1, k1, p1, k1, p1, sm; repeat from * two more times on third needle—18 sts.

Start fourth DPN as follows:

*K2tog, p1, k1, p1, k1, p1, sm; repeat from * three more times on fourth needle—24 sts, or 78 total sts.

Rnd 3: *K2tog, k1, p1, k1, p1, sm; repeat from * two more times on first needle—15 sts.

*K2tog, k1, p1, k1, p1, sm; repeat from * two more times on second needle—15 sts.

*K2tog, k1, p1, k1, p1, sm; repeat from * two more times on third needle—15 sts.

*K2tog, k1, p1, k1, p1, sm; repeat from * three more times on fourth needle—20 sts, or 65 total sts.

Rnd 4: *K2tog, p1, k1, p1, sm; repeat from * two more times on first needle—12 sts.

*K2tog, p1, k1, p1, sm; repeat from * two more times on second needle—12 sts.

*K2tog, p1, k1, p1, sm; repeat from * two more times on third needle—12 sts.

*K2tog, p1, k1, p1, sm; repeat from * three more times on fourth needle—16 sts, or 52 total sts.

Rnd 5: *K2tog, k1, p1, remove marker; repeat from * two more times on first needle—9 sts.

*K2tog, k1, p1, remove marker; repeat from * two more times on second needle—9 sts.

*K2tog, k1, p1, remove marker; repeat from * two more times on third needle—9 sts.

*K2tog, k1, p1, remove marker; repeat from * three more times on fourth needle—12 sts, or 39 total sts.

Rnd 6: *K2tog, p2tog; repeat from * on all needles—26 total sts.

Rnd 7: *K2tog, p2tog; repeat from * on all needles—13 total sts.

Rnd 8: *K2tog, p2tog; repeat from * on all needles, knit last st—7 total sts.

Cut a long tail. With a tapestry needle, pull the yarn through all sts and pull closed. With a tapestry needle, weave in yarn.

SPACE PRINCESS [OPTION 1]

BUNS [MAKE 2]

With size 7 DPNs, CO 15 sts.

Work St st for 18" (46 cm).

DECREASE

Row 1: Ssk, k11, k2tog—13 sts.

Rows 2, 4, 6, and 8: Purl.

Row 3: Ssk, k9, k2tog—11 sts.

Row 5: Ssk, k7, k2tog—9 sts.

Row 7: Ssk, k5, k2tog—7 sts.

BO. Weave in ends with a tapestry needle.

With a tapestry needle, sew the ends together, filling with stuffing as you go. Roll into a spiral (bun) with the seam hidden inside. Sew together every few inches so the spiral stays together. Either pin onto the hat (if you want to use more than one option) or sew onto the hat so they will cover your ears.

ICE PRINCESS [OPTION 2]

BRAIDS (MAKE_3)

With size 7 DPNs, CO 4 sts.

Knit in I-cord for 25" (64 cm).

BO.

Braid all 3 I-cords together and sew the ends together to make a circle.

This can be sewn on the hat so that the braid circles the head like a headband, or pinned onto the hat so that the braid can be altered or left off of the hat altogether.

CLOUD CITY PRINCESS [OPTION 3]

BUN

With one size 7 DPN, CO 9 sts. Divide over 3 DPNs and join.

Rnds 1, 3, 5, 7: Knit around.

Rnd 2: *Kf&b; repeat from * around—18 sts.

Rnd 4: *Kf&b; repeat from * around—36 sts.

Rnd 6: *Kf&b; repeat from * around—72 sts.

Rnd 8: *K5, kf&b; repeat from * around—84 sts.

At this point, you may want to add another DPN and rearrange the stitches so that there are 21 sts on each DPN. Place a marker between the first and second stitch on the first needle to keep track of the beginning of each round.

Knit around for about 3" (8 cm).

DECREASE

Rnd 1: (K2tog) around—42 sts.

Rnd 2: (K2tog) around—21 sts.

Rnd 3: (K2tog) around, ending k1—11 sts.

Cut a long tail. Thread the tail through a tapestry needle and pull through all stitches loosely. Stuff the bun with stuffing and pull the tapestry needle tighter until it is almost closed. Weave in ends.

BRAIDS (MAKE 2)

For each braid, make 3 I-cords.

With size 7 DPNs, CO 4 sts.

Knit in I-cord for 15" (38 cm).

BO and weave in ends.

Braid all 3 I-cords together and sew the ends of the braids together so that they don't come apart. Sew the two ends together so that each braid is shaped like a teardrop.

Sew the bun onto the top of the hat, and sew both teardrop braids to the hat just under the bun.

PADMÉ'S BATTLE CAPE

: DESIGNED BY LINDA J. DUNN

My mother actually designed this cape for a *Star Wars* themed roller derby bout a few years back. She dressed as Padmé in her battle suit and got tons of compliments on her outfit, especially the knit battle cape!

Holding some sway with my mother, I persuaded her to write down the pattern so other *Star Wars* costume lovers can make their own battle outfit!

INSTRUCTIONS

FRONT
BASIC PATTERN STITCH

Starting with the lower edge, CO 150 sts; don't join.

Row 1 (WS): (K1, p1) across.

Row 2: (K1, p1) across.

Row 3: Knit.

Row 4: (K1, p1) across.

Repeat last four rows for a total of six times.

INCREASE ROWS

Row 1: (P1, k1) across.

Row 2: (P1, k1) across.

Row 3: Knit to last st, M1, k1—151 sts.

Row 4: Knit to last st, M1, k1—152 sts.

Row 5: (K1, p1) across.

Row 6: (K1, p1) across.

Row 7: Knit to last st, M1, k1—153 sts.

Row 8: Knit to last st, M1, k1—154 sts.

Work last 8 rows for seven times total, then repeat Rows 1–4—180 sts.

Next row: (K1, p1) across.

Next row: (K1, p1) across.

NECK_OPENING

Row 1 (WS): K80, (left neck side) BO 20, with second skein of yarn knit to end of row (right neck side).

Row 2: Working both neck sides at the same time with separate skeins of yarn, inc 1 st each side edge—81 sts each side.

Row 3: (P1, k1) across left neck, (k1, p1) across right neck.

Row 4: (P1, k1) across right neck, (k1, p1) across left neck.

Row 5: Knit across left neck; for right neck, knit across to last st, M1, k1.

Row 6: Knit across right neck; knit across left neck to last st, M1, k1—82 sts each side.

Row 7: (K1, p1) across left neck, (k1, p1) across right neck.

Row 8: (K1, p1) across right neck, (k1, p1) across left neck.

Row 9: Knit across left neck, knit across right neck to last st, M1, k1.

Row 10: Knit across right neck, knit across left neck to last st, M1, k1—83 sts each side.

Row 11: (P1, k1) across left neck, (p1, k1) across right neck.

Row 12: (P1, k1) across right neck, CO 20, join other side, (p1, k1) across.

Row 13: Knit across.

Row 14: Knit across.

Work Increase Rows 1–8 until there are 182 sts on needle.

Continue Basic Pattern Stitch until cape reaches approximately 48" (122 cm) in length from neck opening. This can be longer if you are tall and shorter if you are vertically challenged. Remember, however, that the cape will stretch, and you don't want it dragging across the floor!

BO all sts when desired length is reached.

: SKILL LEVEL

Intermediate

: FINISHED MEASUREMENTS

Fits men's chest: 40 (43, 48)" [102 (109, 122) cm]

Length: 29¼ (29¼, 30½)" [74 (74, 77) cm]

: MATERIALS

Lion Brand Wool Ease (80% acrylic, 20% wool; 3 oz/85 g; 197 yd/ 180 m): 5 (5, 6) skeins in Black #153 (Color A), and 3 (3, 3) skeins in Cranberry #138 (Color B)

Size 7 (4.5 mm) straight needles

Size 8 (5 mm) straight needles

Size G (4.25 mm) crochet hook

Tapestry needle

: GAUGE

20 stitches and 28 rows = 4" (10cm) in Stockinette stitch on size 8 (5 mm) needles

NEXT GENERATION SWEATER

: DESIGNED BY TONI CARR

When I was a kid, my family and I used to always make time in the week to watch *Star Trek: The Next Generation*. So when it came time to hit the science fiction convention that summer, my mom decided to make us matching Star Trek uniforms. (Despite numerous bribes from my friends, I have made my parents swear that these pictures will never surface.) This sweater is inspired by the cadet-style of uniforms from that show.

INSTRUCTIONS

BACK

With smaller needles and Color A, CO 100 (108, 120) sts.

Work (k2, p2) rib for 3½" (9 cm).

With larger needles, work St st for 18½ (18½, 19)" [47 (47, 48) cm] total from beginning.

SHAPE ARMHOLES

At the beginning of the next 2 rows, BO 4 (5, 7) sts—92 (98, 106) sts.

Change to Color B.

Decrease one stitch at each edge every RS row EOR 2 (4, 4) times—88,(90, 98) sts remain.

Continue St st until armhole measures 7½ (8¼, 8¼)" [19 (21, 21) cm] from beginning.

At the beginning of each of the next 10 (6, 10) rows, BO 6 (10, 6) sts—28 (36, 38) sts.

NECK

At the beginning of the next 6 rows, BO 2 sts.

BO remaining 16 (18, 26) sts.

FRONT

Work same as back.

SLEEVES (MAKE 2)

With Color A and smaller needles, CO 48 (48, 52) sts.

Work (k2, p2) rib for 2" (5 cm).

Change to larger needles.

Work 2" (5 cm) St st, ending on a purl row—4" (10 cm) total from beginning.

BEGIN INCREASES

Row 1: K1, M1, knit to last st, M1, k1.

Row 2: Purl.

Row 3: Knit.

Row 4: Purl.

Row 5: Knit.

Row 6: Purl.

Work last 6 rows a total of ten times—68 (68, 72) sts.

Continue in St st until piece measures 16 (16, 16½)" [41 (41, 42) cm] from beginning, ending on a purl row.

Next row: With Color A, k33 (33, 35); with Color B, k2; with Color A, k33 (33, 35).

Next row: With Color A, p32 (32, 34); with Color B, p4; with Color A, p32 (32, 34).

Next row: With Color A, k31 (31, 33); with Color B, k6; with Color A, k31 (31, 33).

Next row: With Color A, p30 (30, 32); with Color B, p8; with Color A, p30 (30, 32).

Continue in this manner, turning one Color A stitch into Color B on each side of the sleeve until all stitches in Color A are now Color B.

AT THE SAME TIME: When there are 36 (36, 40) sts in Color B, begin shaping sleeves as follows:

At beginning of next 2 rows, BO 4 (5, 7) sts—60 (58, 58) sts.

Next row: Sl 1, k2tog, knit to last 3 sts, ssk, k1—58 (56, 56) sts.

Next row: Purl.

Repeat last 2 rows 14 (16, 16) times more—30 (24, 24) sts.

Next row: Sl1, k2tog, knit to last 3 sts, ssk, k1.

Next row: P1, p2tog, purl to last 3 sts, p2tog, p1.

Repeat last 2 rows once more.

Beginning of next 4 rows, BO 2 sts.

BO 14 (8, 8) remaining sts.

FINISHING

Seam the sides of the body to the armholes and seam the sleeves to where you began shaping. Attach the sleeves to the shoulders of the sweater. Seam along the top of the shoulders to the neck, and bind off. With the crochet hook, work one row of slip stitch around the neck for a neat finish.

TREK GIRL DRESS

: DESIGNED BY TONI CARR

The mini dress uniform, worn in both the classic *Star Trek* and the rebooted movie, is a definite must-have for any girl wanting to dress up like her favorite female *Star Trek* character! This classic red dress is based on the uniforms worn in the J.J. Abrams movie. Pair it with a black shirt, communicator pin, and black boots and voilà! Instant costume for the convention! The best part is that this dress is cute enough and comfortable enough to be worn for a regular night out (with no Vulcans involved)!

Knit in a cotton/linen blend yarn, it's very comfortable to work with and wear. And since it's worked almost entirely in one piece, with only some slight decreasing and increasing, you'll knit this up faster than you can say, "Warp speed, Captain!"

INSTRUCTIONS

With circular needle, CO 1 st, pm, CO 18 (22, 24, 28) sts, pm, CO 33 (37, 39, 43) sts, pm, CO 18 (22, 24, 28) sts, pm, CO 1 st—71 (83, 89, 101) sts. Do not join.

Row 1 (WS): Purl.

Row 2 (RS): Kf&b in first st, sm, M1, knit to marker, M1, sm, k1, M1, knit to marker, M1, sm, k1, M1, knit to marker, M1, sm, kf&b—79 (91, 97, 109) sts.

Row 3: Purl.

Row 4 (to increase 12 sts): Kf&b in first st, k1, M1, sm; *k1, M1, knit to marker, M1, sm, k1, M1; repeat from * twice more, ending sm, k1, kf&b in last st—91 (103, 109, 121) sts.

Row 5: Purl.

Row 6: K1, kf&b in second st, knit to marker, M1, sm; *k1, M1, knit to marker, M1, sm; repeat from * twice more, k1, M1, kf&b in next st, k1—101 (113, 119, 131) sts.

Row 7: Purl.

Repeat Rows 6 and 7 for 9 (10, 10, 11) more times—191 (213, 219, 241) sts.

SET UP FOR ROUNDS

Using cable cast on, CO 4 (4, 4, 4) sts; *knit to marker, M1, sm, k1, M1; repeat from * to end—203 (225, 231, 253) sts.

With RS facing, join, k2, place new marker to show where joined. *(Note: It's helpful if the new marker is not the same as the other markers you are using, as it marks the beginning of your row.)*

Rnd 1: Knit around.

Rnd 2: Skipping joining marker, *knit to next marker, M1, sm, k1, M1; repeat from * three times more—211 (233, 239, 261) sts.

Rnds 3–18: Repeat Rnds 1 and 2—275 (297, 303, 325) sts.

Next rnd: Knit around.

SET UP FOR BODY

*Knit to second marker, remove marker, place 56 (62, 64, 70) sts on waste yarn for sleeve; repeat from * again. Knit to end of rnd. Repeat for other sleeve.

Knit around for 3" (8 cm) on 163 (173, 175, 185) sts.

DECREASE ROUND

Knit to last 3 sts before side marker, k2tog, k1, sm, k1, ssk, knit to last 3 sts before next side marker, k2tog, k1, sm, k1, ssk, knit to end—159 (169, 171, 181) sts.

Knit 30 rnds.

Repeat Decrease Round—155 (165, 167, 177) sts.

Knit 40 rnds.

INCREASE ROUND

Rnd 1: Knit to last st before marker, M1, k1, sm, k1, M1, repeat with other marker—159 (169, 171, 181) sts.

Rnds 2–6: Knit.

Rnd 7: Repeat Rnd 1—163 (173, 175, 185) sts.

Knit 3 rnds.

Next rnd: Repeat Rnd 1—167 (177, 179, 189) sts.

Repeat last 4 rnds 17 (19, 20, 22) times total—235 (253, 259, 277) sts.

Knit even for 2 (3, 4, 4)" [5 (8, 10, 10) cm] or to desired length.

Purl 2 rnds.

BO.

SLEEVES

Place sts from one sleeve on waste yarn onto DPN, pick up 5 (6, 6, 7) sts from body of sweater, pm, and join—61 (68, 70, 77) sts.

Purl 2 rnds.

BO.

Repeat for second sleeve.

Weave in all ends.

TROUBLESOME TOY

: DESIGNED BY TONI CARR

I remember watching the original *Star Trek* and falling in love with the pesky little tribbles that invaded the ship. OF COURSE I wanted my own, but we could never find a toy tribble!

Now you can knit one of your very own! Stuff it with a squeaker, or if you want to drive your cats crazy, fill it with catnip when you stuff it!

INSTRUCTIONS

CO 6 sts; divide onto 3 needles, pm, and join.

Rnd 1: Knit around.

Rnd 2: Kf&b each st around—12 sts.

Rnd 3: Knit around.

Rnd 4: Kf&b each st around—24 sts.

Rnd 5: Knit around.

Rnd 6: (K1, kf&b) around—36 sts.

Rnd 7: Knit.

Rnd 8: (K2, kf&b) around—48 sts.

Rnds 9–14: Knit.

Rnd 15: (K2, k2tog) around—36 sts.

Rnd 16: Knit.

Rnd 17: (K1, k2tog) around—24 sts.

: SKILL LEVEL

Intermediate

: FINISHED MEASUREMENT

About 4" (10 cm) in diameter

: MATERIALS

Knit Picks Suri Dream Hand Dyed (74% Suri Alpaca, 22% Peruvian highland wool, 4% nylon; 50 g/143 yd): 1 skein in #24233 Aquatic

Four size 8 (5 mm) double-pointed needles

Ring-type stitch markers

: GAUGE

1–2 stitches = 1" (3 cm) in Stockinette stitch on size 8 (5 mm) needles

Rnd 18: Knit.

Rnd 19: (K2tog) around—12 sts.

Rnd 20: Knit.

(K2tog) around until 3 sts remain.

Cut yarn and pull through remaining stitches.

FINISHING

Take a hairbrush to the yarn and "fluff" your tribble!

: SHILL LEVEL

Advanced

: FINISHED MEASUREMENT

16" (41 cm) tall

: MATERIALS

Caron Simply Soft Heather (100% acrylic; 6 oz/170 g, 315 yd): 1 skein in #9742 Grey Heather (MC)

Caron Simply Soft Brites (100% acrylic; 6 oz/ 170 g, 315 yd): 1 skein in #9611 Rose Violet (CC)

Two small craft eyes

Toy stuffing

Size 3 (3.25 mm) 32" (81 cm) circular needle

One size 3 (3.25 mm) double-pointed needle, for three-needle bind off

Stitch markers

Stitch holder

Tapestry needle

: GAUGE

26 stitches and 8 rows = 4" (10cm) in Stockinette stitch on size 3 (3.25 mm) needles

ROBOT OF THE FUTURE

: DESIGNED BY MARILEE NORRIS

You'll definitely want to knit up this adorable cyborg! He's got a knitted brain peeking out of the top of his head, and he's not afraid to use it. Originally inspired by the classic Cybermen of *Doctor Who*, he's undergone a bit of an evolution (a much cuter evolution). His plans to dominate mankind might be thwarted by his cuteness, so he needs to work extra hard at being evil. His secret plan is to take over your household, and then . . . *the world*.

SPECIAL INSTRUCTIONS

It's important that you stuff your robot as you knit it.

INSTRUCTIONS

BODY

Note: The robot's body is knit from the crotch up.

With MC, CO 8 sts using the backward loop cast on (page 124).

Row 1 (RS): Kf&b, knit to last 2 sts before the end of the row, kf&b, k1—10 sts.

Row 2: Purl.

Repeat Rows 1 and 2 until you have 26 sts on the needle, ending with a WS row. Break yarn and transfer sts to a stitch holder.

With RS facing you, pick up 8 sts from the cast-on edge and repeat Rows 1 and 2 until 26 sts are on the needle, ending with a RS row.

Fold the work in half so all live stitches are at the top, and right sides are facing out (it will look just like a little pair of underwear). The stitches just finished being knit should be in the back and the stitches still on the stitch holder should be in the front. Using the circular needle, place the stitches from the stitch holder back onto the needles. Prepare to knit in the round, remembering to place a stitch marker to designate the beginning of the round and another on the front of the robot's body.

Knit every rnd in St st until you reach 4" (10 cm) from the cast-on edge.

Rnd 1: P26, k26.

Rnds 2–3: Knit.

Repeat Rnds 1-3 twice more.

Knit every rnd until you reach 6" (15 cm) from the cast-on edge.

Using the three-needle bind off (page 122) across 8 stitches, seam closed the robot's left shoulder (the front of the robot's body should be facing you). Break yarn. Place the center 10 stitches of the front and back needle onto stitch holder (20 stitches in all). These live stitches will later be picked up to create the robot's head. Attach new yarn and seam the remaining 8 stitches closed for the robot's right shoulder using the three-needle bind off.

HEAD

Pick up the 20 live stitches from the robot's body and distribute the stitches evenly over the two needles for magic loop knitting (page 66).

Place a stitch marker and prepare to knit in the round. Join new yarn for the head.

Rnd 1: Purl.

Rnd 2: Kf&b, k1; repeat to end of rnd—11 sts each needle.

Rnd 3: Knit.

Rnd 4: *Kf&b, knit to last 2 stitches before the end of the needle, kf&b, k1; repeat from * one time to the end of the rnd—2 sts are added to each needle—13 sts each needle.

Repeat Rnds 3 and 4 until there are a total of 25 sts on each needle.

Knit next 15 rnds.

BO and leave a long tail for seaming.

BRAIN

With CC and circular needle, CO 200 sts.

Immediately BO, and break yarn, leaving a long tail.

Using a tapestry needle, weave the yarn in and out along the CO edge every 1" (3 cm) or so in a long running stitch. Gently pull on the knitted yarn, gathering it together so it bends back and forth, creating the "folds" of the brain. Place a couple of small stitches throughout to help the brain take shape and weave in ends.

ARMS (MAKE 2)

Note: The arms are made from the hands up.

With MC, CO 10 sts using the backward loop cast on. Distribute stitches evenly across the two needles for magic loop knitting (instructions follow). Prepare to knit in the round. Place a stitch marker to designate the beginning of the round.

Rnd 1: *Kf&b, knit to last 2 stitches before the end of the needle, kf&b, k1; repeat from * one time to end of rnd—7 sts each needle.

Rnd 2: Knit.

Rnds 3–6: Repeat Rnds 1 and 2 for two more times—11 sts each needle.

Rnds 7–10: Knit.

Rnd 11a (*right arm only*): K7; place the next 4 sts onto a piece of stitch holder; CO 4 sts; knit to end of rnd.

Rnd 11b (*left arm only*): Knit 11; place the next 4 sts onto a piece of stitch holder; CO 4 sts; knit to end of rnd.

Rnds 12–15: Knit.

Rnd 16: Purl.

Rnds 17–18: Knit. (*Note: Slip the first stitch of Rnd 17.*)

Rnd 19: Purl.

Rnds 20–37: Knit. (*Note: Slip the first stitch of Rnd 20.*)

Rnds 38–41: Repeat Rnds 16–19 one time.

Rnds 42–73: Knit. (*Note: Slip the first stitch of Rnd 42.*)

Leave the last 1" (3 cm) of the arm unstuffed. BO using the three-needle bind off. Seam the tip of the hand closed.

THUMB

Place the 4 stitches from the scrap yarn onto your needle, and pick up 4 stitches around the thumb opening, making sure the stitches are evenly divided for magic loop knitting.

Knit 6 rnds.

BO using the three-needle bind off.

ARM DETAIL (MAKE 2)

With MC, CO 3 sts.

Knit 2 rows in St st.

Knit I-cord until you reach 2½" (6 cm) from the cast-on edge.

Turn work so the working yarn is on the right, and purl 1 row.

BO and leave a long tail for sewing onto the robot's arm.

LEGS (MAKE 2)

Note: The robot's legs are made from the top down, knit back and forth to shape the thigh and then joined to knit in the round for the rest of the leg. The foot is knit classic sock style, using short rows to shape the heel.

With MC, CO 4 sts.

Rows 1, 5, 9, and 13 (RS): Kf&b, knit to 2 stitches before the end of the row, kf&b, k1.

Row 2 (and all even rnds): Purl.

Row 3: (Kf&b, k1) three times—9 sts.

Row 7: Kf&b, k4, kf&b, k3, kf&b, k1—14 sts.

Row 11: (Kf&b, k2) four times; kf&b, k1— 19 sts.

Row 15: (Kf&b, k3) four times, kf&b, k2— 24 sts.

Row 17: K24.

Fold work in half so right sides are facing out. Prepare to knit in the round by arranging the work so that the stitches are divided evenly on two needles. Join to knit in the round. Mark the beginning of the round with a stitch marker.

Rnds 18–19: Knit.

Rnd 20: (K1, k2tog, k9) twice—11 sts on each needle.

Rnds 21–32: Knit.

Rnd 33: Purl.

Rnds 34–35: Knit. (*Note: Slip the first stitch of Rnd 34.*)

Rnd 36: Purl.

Rnds 37–51: Knit. (*Note: Slip the first stitch of Rnd 37.*)

Rnd 52–55: Repeat Rnds 33–36 one time.

Rnds 56–61: Knit. (*Note: Slip the first stitch of Rnd 56.*)

Right Leg Only: K11. Turn to the back side of the round. You will now be knitting back and forth along the back of the work to form the heel. Proceed to Turning the Heel.

Left Leg Only: Proceed directly to Turning the Heel.

TURNING THE HEEL

To wrap and turn (w&t) on a knit row: Bring yarn forward between the needles, slip the stitch to the right-hand needle, bring yarn around the stitch to the back of your work, slip the stitch back to the left-hand needle, and turn work.

To w&t on a purl row: Bring yarn between needles to the back of your work, slip the stitch to the right-hand needle, bring yarn around the stitch to the front of the work, slip the stitch back to the left-hand needle, and turn work.

When knitting or purling wrapped stitches: Slip the wrapped stitch to the right-hand needle and use the left-hand needle to pick up the wrap. Place the wrap on the right-hand needle beside the stitch. Knit or purl the stitch together with the wrap.

When knitting or purling double wrapped stitches: Knit or purl the stitch in the same way as you would a wrapped stitch. However, instead of picking up one wrap, you'll pick up two.

Row 62: K10, w&t.

Row 63: P9, w&t.

Row 64: K8, w&t.

Row 65: P7, w&t.

Row 66: K6, w&t.

Row 67: P5, w&t.

Row 68: K5, knit wrapped st, w&t.

Row 69: Sl 1, p5, purl wrapped stitch, w&t.

Row 70: Sl 1, k6, knit double wrapped stitch, w&t.

Row 71: Sl 1, p7, purl double wrapped stitch, w&t.

Row 72: Sl 1, k8, knit double wrapped stitch. Do not turn work.

Resume working in the round.

Rnds 73–80: Knit. (*Note: On the last stitch of the first round, remember to work the last stitch by knitting it together with the double wraps.*)

Rnd 81: P11, k11.

Rnds 82–83: Knit.

Rnd 84: P11, k11.

Rnd 85: Knit.

Rnd 86: (K1, k2tog, k5, k2tog, k1) twice— 9 sts each needle.

Rnd 87: P9, k9.

Cut yarn and close end of robot boot using the Kitchener stitch.

FINISHING

Make sure that all parts of the robot are lightly stuffed. Sew the eyes to the robot's face and place the brain on top of the robot's head. Using gray yarn, sew the brain in place with an overcast stitch around the top of the robot's head.

Sew arm detail in place on the upper arm; repeat for the other arm. Gently fold the top of the arms over the edge of the shoulders and sew in place.

Sew the legs in place. Weave in all ends.

Now you've got yourself a dark but adorably cute evildoer who's on the lookout for more body parts to salvage!

MAGIC LOOP INSTRUCTIONS

Magic Loop is great for knitting anything you want into a tube—socks, gloves, hats—without ever using double-pointed needles! The method is very simple once you get going! You're simply "splitting" your stitches through a long circular needle by pulling the cable through the middle of those stitches.

1. With your 32" circular needle, cast on the required number of stitches.

2. Hold the needle with the working yarn in your right hand. About halfway through your cast-on stitches, bend the cable of your circular needle and pull it out between the stitches.

3. Slide the stitches onto the two needles (half on one needle, half on the other).

4. Hold the two needles up. The needle closest to you is now your front needle. The needle farthest away is your back needle. Make sure the tail of your yarn is on the back needle and the working yarn is on the front needle.

5. Knit the stitches on your front on the first needle (just like you would knit stitches on straight needles!). When you reach the end, you have knit half a round. Point both needle tips to the right, and slide the front needle (This WAS your back needle, but you've now moved it to the front.) into the stitches that are on the cable.

6. Slide the stitches you have just knit onto the cable. Knit the second half of your round.

7. Continue knitting around.

: SKILL LEVEL

Easy

: FINISHED MEASUREMENTS

10½' (3¾ m) long by 3"
(8 cm) wide

: MATERIALS

Plymouth Encore Worsted
(75% acrylic, 25% wool;
100g/200 yd): 2 skeins
each in #3335 Lime Green
(Color A), #0215 Yellow
(Color B), #0449 Pink
(Color C), #0180 Hot
Pink (Color D), #0455
Pale Blue (Color E),
#4045 Bright Blue
(Color F)

Size 8 (5 mm) straight
needles

: GAUGE

20 stitches and 22 rows
= 4" (10 cm) in garter
stitch on size 8 (5mm)
needles

TIME TRAVELER SCARF

: DESIGNED BY TONI CARR

There's nothing more recognizable for sci-fi
fans than a certain 20-foot-long multicolored
scarf! This version is a slightly more
manageable nod to the famous one from the
'70s.

Knit in fun, bright colors and still incredibly
long, this skinny scarf is a great accessory
to any outfit! Or do what a friend and I did at
Inconjunction one summer and hold a "How to
Knit" panel to teach a bunch of sci-fi lovers to
make their own scarf. Not only will you spread
your love of knitting, but you'll also make some
great new friends in the process!

INSTRUCTIONS

CO 15 sts.

In g stitch, work the first stripe pattern two times.

Color A: 16 rows

Color B: 2 rows

Color A: 2 rows

Color D: 8 rows

Color F: 24 rows

Color B: 4 rows

Color C: 8 rows

Color E: 8 rows

Color D: 6 rows

Color B: 8 rows

Continuing in g st, work the second stripe pattern one time.

Color B: 8 rows

Color A: 16 rows

Color B: 2 rows

Color D: 8 rows

Color E: 2 rows

Color B: 24 rows

Color F: 4 rows

Color C: 6 rows

Color D: 8 rows

Color A: 8 rows

Work the first stripe pattern once more.

Work the second stripe pattern twice more.

Work the first stripe pattern three times more.

BO.

AIM TO MISBEHAVE BROWN JACKET

: DESIGNED BY TONI CARR

Firefly is easily one of my favorite television shows of all time. It's a mix of gun-slinging Western and futuristic sci-fi!

This jacket is inspired by the show and the characters of Malcolm and Zoe. Being rebels, a.k.a. "Browncoats," this jacket of course has to be brown, but I thought it would be fun to make a feminine version of the traditional costumes from the show.

Lace edging on the bottom of the coat and the sleeves gives the jacket a lot of movement. It's light enough to wear whether you need to run from the Alliance or just curl up on the couch for a *Firefly* marathon with your fellow Browncoats!

INSTRUCTIONS

SLEEVES (MAKE 2)

CO 74 (74, 86, 86) sts.

Work in g st for 8 rows.

LACE PATTERN

(*Note: Slip the sl 1 sts as if to knit.*)

Row 1 (RS): K1; *sl 1, k1, psso, k3, yo, k1, yo, k3, k2tog, p1; repeat from * to last st, k1.

Row 2 (and all WS rows): Purl.

Row 3: K1; *sl 1, k1, psso, k2, yo, k3, yo, k2, k2tog, p1; repeat from * to last st, k1.

Row 5: K1; *sl 1, k1, psso, k1, yo, k5, yo, k1, k2tog, p1; repeat from * to last st, k1.

Row 7: K1; *yo, k3, k2tog, k1, sl 1, k1, psso, k3, yo, p1; repeat from * to last st, k1.

Row 9: K1; *k1, yo, k2, k2tog, k1, sl 1, k1, psso, k2, yo, k1, p1; repeat from * to last st, k1.

Row 11: K1; *k2, yo, k1, k2tog, k1, sl 1, k1, psso, k1, yo, k2, p1; repeat from * to last st, k1.

Row 12: Purl.

Work in St st for 8 rows.

DECREASE ROWS

Row 1 (RS): K1, k2tog, knit to last 3 sts, ssk, k1.

Row 2: Purl.

Row 3: Knit.

Row 4: Purl.

Repeat last 4 rows 5 (2, 5, 1) times—64 (70, 76, 84) sts remain.

Continue in St st until sleeve is a total of 14" (36 cm) from beginning, ending with a purl row.

INCREASE ROWS

Row 1: K1, M1, knit to last st, M1, k1.

Row 2: Purl.

Row 3: Knit.

Row 4: Purl.

Row 5: Knit.

Row 6: Purl.

Row 7: Knit.

Row 8: Purl.

Repeat last 8 rows seven times—78 (84, 90, 98) sts remain.

Continue in St st until sleeve measures 20¾" (53 cm) from beginning, ending WS.

BO 9 (10, 11, 12) sts at the beginning of the next 2 rows.

Place remaining 60 (64, 68, 74) sts on holder.

BODY

CO 223 (247, 271, 295) sts.

Work in g st for 8 rows.

LACE PATTERN

Row 1 (RS): K9, p1; *sl 1, k1, psso, k3, yo, k1, yo, k3, k2tog, p1; repeat from * to last 9 sts, knit to end.

Row 2 (and all WS rows): K6, purl to last 6 sts, k6.

Row 3: K9, p1, *sl 1, k1, psso, k2, yo, k3, yo, k2, k2tog, p1; repeat from * to last 9 sts, k9.

Row 5: K9, p1, *sl 1, k1, psso, k1, yo, k5, yo, k1, k2tog, p1; repeat from * to last 9 sts, k9.

Row 7: K9, p1, *yo, k3, k2tog, k1, sl 1, k1, psso, k3, yo, p1; repeat from * to last 9 sts, k9.

Row 9: K9, p1, *k1, yo, k2, k2tog, k1, sl1, k1, psso, k2, yo, k1, p1; repeat from * to last 9 sts, k9.

Row 11: K9, p1, *k2, yo, k1, k2tog, k1, sl 1, k1, psso, k1, yo, k2, p1; repeat from * to last 9 sts, k9.

Repeat Rows 1–12 ten times.

Keeping 6 sts each edge in g st, work in St st until piece measures 19" (48 cm) from beginning, ending RS.

BUTTONHOLES

Row 1 (WS): K6, purl to last 6 sts, BO 3, knit to end.

Row 2: CO 3 sts over buttonhole, knit across.

Work 24 rows even; repeat Rows 1–2 for buttonhole rows.

Repeat last 26 rows three times more.

Note: Maintain established buttonhole rows for remainder of pattern (seven buttonholes total). At the same time, when piece measures 29 (28½, 28, 27½)" [74 (72, 71, 70) cm] from beginning end with a WS row.

DIVIDE FOR FRONT AND BACK

Next row: K6, p42 (47, 53, 57) for left front.

BO 18 (20, 22, 24) sts for underarm. P91 (101, 109, 121) across back, BO 18 (20, 20, 20) sts for right underarm, purl to last 6 sts, k6.

Next row: Knit across right front, pm, knit across sts from holder for right sleeve, pm, knit across back, pm, knit across sts from holder for left sleeve, pm, knit across left front—307 (335, 363, 395) sts.

Row 1 (WS): K6, purl across, ending k6.

Row 2 (RS): *Knit to last 2 sts before marker, ssk, sm, k2tog; rep from * three times more, ending knit to end of row—8 sts decreased.

Repeat last 2 rows until 177 (195, 213, 235) sts remain.

Work Row 1 again.

Knit across and decrease 6 (9, 6, 9) sts even on each sleeve—165 (177, 201, 223) sts.

BORDER

Knit 3 rows.

Next row (RS): K2, BO 3, knit to end.

Next row: Knit across and CO 3 sts over buttonhole.

Knit 3 rows.

BO.

FINISHING

Join sleeve seams. Sew on the buttons opposite to the buttonholes.

73

QUESTION:

While Tribbles are surely trouble, in what way were they helpful on the *Enterprise*?

A. They alerted the ship to a cargo hold full of poisoned grain.
B. They soothed Captain Kirk's cranky mood.
C. They helped steer the ship to safety.

Answer: A. Some Tribbles got into the grain and died, alerting the crew that it was poisoned!

SECTION_3

COMICS AND
MANGA

SKILL LEVEL

Intermediate

SIZE

One size fits all (see Special Instructions)

FINISHED MEASUREMENTS

20½" (52 cm) long and 8" (20 cm) circumference on relaxed rib (rib stretches to fit 14 to 15" [36 to 38 cm])

MATERIALS

Plymouth Encore Worsted (75% Acrylic, 25% Wool; 100 g/200 yd): 1 skein each in #217 Black (MC) and 1 skein #1385 Fuchsia (CC)

2 yards (2m) rainbow elastic (optional)

Five size 8 (5 mm) double-pointed needles

One size 8 (5 mm) 16" (41 cm) circular needle

Stitch markers

GAUGE

20 stitches and 26 rows = 4" (10cm) in Stockinette stitch on size 8 (5 mm) needles

SUPER AWESOME FANTASTIC MEGA SUPER CUTE MANGA LEG WARMERS

: DESIGNED BY TONI CARR

Japanese Manga comics have always been a favorite of mine—not only for the great stories, but also for the awesome styling and fashion that is so high energy and eclectic it could only come from Japan! The Manga costumes are always a big hit at conventions, but there is also quite a bit of this style stepping out into everyday life as well.

A quick knit, these leg warmers are totally influenced by that Japanese fashion! They're tight at the knee with a big bell at the foot. Pair these with really chunky boots and a pleated skirt for an Amu Hinamori look or pair them with short shorts, fishnets, and gloves for a street goth/punk style!

SPECIAL INSTRUCTIONS

Gals with skinny legs may find knitting in a little thread of rainbow elastic at the top helpful. To add elastic, simply hold the rainbow elastic thread with your yarn as you work the top rib rows.

INSTRUCTIONS

Beginning at the top, CO 48 sts with MC. Pm and join to work in the round, dividing sts evenly onto three needles.

Work (k1, p1) rib for 1½" (4 cm). Knit 1 rnd.

Rnd 1 (Increase Round): K1, M1, knit to 1 st before end of needle, M1, k1. Repeat for each needle—54 sts.

Rnd 2: Knit.

Rnd 3: Knit.

Rnd 4: Repeat Increase Round—60 sts.

Change to CC.

Rnds 1–8: Knit.

Rnd 9: Repeat Increase Round—66 sts.

Note: You may need to switch to the circular needle before completing increases. Simply place stitch markers where the beginnings and ends of the DPN would be to track where your increases should go.

Repeat last 9 rows until 126 sts are on the needles.

Change to circular needle with stitch marker placed at beginning of rnd.

Knit every rnd in St st until piece from first CC rnd measures 20¾" (53 cm).

Change to MC and knit every rnd for 6½" (17 cm).

BO.

Weave in all ends.

Repeat for second leg warmer.

: SKILL LEVEL

Advanced

: FINISHED MEASUREMENTS

S = calf circumference
12–14" (30–36 cm)

M = calf circumference
14–16" (36–41 cm)

L = calf circumference
16–18" (41–46 cm)

: MATERIALS

Knit Picks Stroll Sport
Sock Yarn (75% superwash
Merino wool, 25% nylon;
50 g/137 yd): 3 (3, 4)
skeins in #24701 Black
(MC), and 1 skein each
in #25055 Blue Topaz
(Color A); #25049
Passionfruit pink (Color
B); #25052 Peapod (Color
C); #25054 Pageant
purple (Color D)

Five size 2 (2.75 mm)
double-pointed needles

Five size 3 (3.25 mm)
double-pointed needles

Stitch markers

Tapestry needle

Yarn needle

: GAUGE

27 stitches and 28 rows
equals 4" in Stockinette
stitch on size 3 (3.25
mm) needles

TANK GIRL SOCKS

: DESIGNED BY LAURA HOHMAN

Tank Girl was hands-down one of my favorite comics and movies as a teenager! These socks are inspired by the bright colors and crazy style of the comic book.

INSTRUCTIONS

CUFF

With MC and size 2 DPNs, CO 72 (80, 92) sts, join, and work in (k2, p2) rib for 2" (5 cm).

BODY

Change to size 3 DPNs and knit 1 rnd, ending, M1 after last st—73 (81, 93) sts.

Knit Rnds 1–32 of Chart I, knitting last st of each rnd with MC.

Rnd 33 (Decrease Round): K2tog, knit to last 3 sts, ssk, k1 in MC—71 (79, 91) sts.

Continue knitting Chart I pattern (ending each round with k1 in MC), working a decrease round every four rounds until 49 (53, 61) sts remain. *(Note: For legs less than 14" [36 cm] from knee to heel, work decrease round every 3 three rounds.)*

Continue knitting even rounds of Chart I pattern (ending each round with k1 in MC) until desired leg length is reached. For last st of final round, k2tog with MC—48 (52, 60) sts.

Note: You will abandon the main pattern for now and pick it back up again when knitting the instep.

HEEL

K12 (13, 15) sts with MC.

Sl 12 (13, 15) sts from previous needle onto same needle.

There should now be 24 (26, 30) sts on this needle for heel.

Remaining 24 (26, 30) sts for instep should be split between two needles and ignored for now.

Work heel sts back and forth with MC as follows:

Row 1: Sl 1 as if to purl, purl across.

Row 2 (RS): *Sl 1 as if to purl, k1; repeat from * across.

Work Rows 1 and 2 until heel measures 2½" (6 cm), ending RS.

TURN HEEL

Work a series of short rows from center of heel:

Row 1: Sl 1, p12 (14, 16), p2tog, p1, turn.

Row 2: Sl 1, k5, ssk, k1, turn.

Row 3: Sl 1, p6, p2tog, p1, turn.

Row 4: Sl 1, k7, ssk, k1, turn.

Repeat (increasing number of sts purl or knit each row), until all sts have been added to row.

There should be 15 (16, 18) sts remaining. End heel on a knit row, working an extra row if necessary.

INSTEP

Pick up and k13 (14, 15) sts on side of heel flap with spare needle, starting Chart II pattern that matches up with where you need to pick up

knitting the Chart I pattern on the instep. Last knit stitch should be with MC.

K24 (26, 30) sts (held in reserve for instep) onto second needle, working a continuation of the Chart I pattern from where you ended on the leg.

Pick up and k12 (14, 15) sts on other side of heel flap with third needle and knit 8 (8, 9) heel sts onto same needle in Chart II pattern. First knit stitch should be with MC.

Place stitch marker on first needle and then slip other 7 (8, 9) heel sts onto end of first needle. *Note: Stitch marker notes end of round for pattern knitting.*

There should be a total of 64 (70, 78) sts on 3 needles. Needles 1 and 3 should have 20 (22, 24) sts.

Needle 2 should have 24 (26, 30) sts.

Note: Continue working rest of instep following appropriate patterns. Chart I on second needle and Chart II on first and third needles.

DECREASE ROUND

Needle 1: Knit to within 3 sts of end, ssk, k1 in MC.

Needle 2: Knit.

Needle 3: K1 in MC, k2tog, knit to end.

EVEN ROUND

Needle 1: Knit to within 1 st of end, k1 in MC.

Needle 2: Knit.

Needle 3: K1 in MC, knit to end.

Repeat Decrease Round and Even Round until 48 (52, 60) sts remain.

First and third needles should have 12 (13, 15) sts and second needle should have 24 (26, 30) sts. Knit around until foot measures 2" (5 cm) less than desired length.

TOE

Change to MC only. Knit 1 rnd.

DECREASE ROUND

Needle 1: Knit to last 3 sts, k2tog, k1.

Needle 2: K1, ssk, knit to last 3 sts, k2tog, k1.

Needle 3: K1, ssk, knit to end.

Repeat 1 rnd knit, 1 Decrease Round until 16 (20, 20) sts remain.

Knit remaining sts from first needle onto third needle. You should now have 8 (10, 10) sts on each needle. Cut a 12" (30 cm) tail of MC and thread onto a yarn needle. Hold sock with yarn at RS, tail coming from the rear needle. Finish toe using Kitchener stitch.

Use a tapestry needle to pull the tail through the end of the sock.

CHART 1   CHART 2   MAIN PATTERN: Bottom Instep Pattern

COLOR_KEY

MC = Black
A = Blue Topaz
B = Passionfruit
C = Peapod
D = Pageant

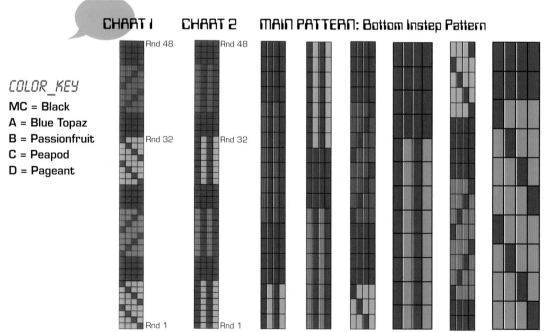

Rnd 48 ... Rnd 32 ... Rnd 1

TOP THIS FASCINATOR

: DESIGNED BY TONI CARR

This mini fascinator top hat is a nod to the
trendy style sported by Death in The Sandman
comic series and *Death: The High Cost of
Living*. Sassy and trendy, you would never see
her in drab robes or carrying a scythe! Knit
in the round with only a few increases and
decreases for shaping, this pattern is very
quick to make. It is felted to hold a solid shape,
then accented with a veil, feathers, or anything
else you decide to use to decorate it!

INSTRUCTIONS

CO 48 sts, pm, and join.

Rnds 1–9: Knit.

Rnd 10: (K6, k2tog) around—42 sts.

Rnd 11: Knit.

Rnd 12: (K8, k2tog) around, ending k2—38 sts.

Rnds 13–35: Knit.

Rnd 36: (K7, M1) around, ending k3—43 sts.

Rnd 37: Knit.

Rnd 38: (K5, M1) around, ending k3—51 sts.

Rnd 39: Knit.

Rnd 40: (K8, k2tog) around, ending k1—46 sts.

Rnd 41: (K2tog) around to last 6 sts, k4, k2tog—25 sts.

Rnd 42: (K2tog) around to last 5 sts, k3, k2tog—14 sts.

Rnd 43: (K2tog) around to last 4 sts, k2, k2tog—8 sts.

Rnd 44: (K2tog) around to last 2 sts, k2—4 sts.

FINISHING

Cut the yarn, thread it through a tapestry needle, weave it through the remaining stitches, and close.

Wash the hat in really hot, sudsy water to felt (page 125), then stuff it with plastic bags or towels to block. Let the bottom brim roll up. With the increases at the top, you can even set the top at an angle for a cool off-kilter look.

Sew on the netting for the veil. Get as creative as you want at this point! Add felt flowers, feathers, etc.! Use some bobby pins to hold the hat in place on your head, or sew on a comb or hair clips.

HEY! FYI!

Awesome geek Wil Wheaton is not only an actor on *Star Trek*, *The Guild*, *The Big Bang Theory*, and *Eureka* (all nerd staples), he's a writer as well! He has written several books, including *Just a Geek*, which features an introduction from Neil Gaiman!

SKILL LEVEL

Intermediate

FINISHED MEASUREMENT

5" (8 cm) tall after light felting

MATERIALS

Knit Picks Wool of the Andes (100% Peruvian Highland wool; 50 g/ 110 yd): 1 skein in #25075 Rouge

One ½" (4 cm) diameter black button

One ¼" (3 cm) diameter black button

Stuffing

Four size 6 (4 mm) double-pointed needles

Stitch marker

Two stitch holders

Sewing needle and black thread

GAUGE

20 stitches and 21 rows = 4" (10 cm) in Stockinette stitch on size 6 (4 mm) needles

CREEPY FILLER BUNNY

: DESIGNED BY TONI CARR

I always loved the demented world of Jhonen Vasquez. In one of his comics, Vasquez introduced the concept of a creepy, lab-created bunny called Filler Bunny, which he used when running into a deadline and needed filler material for his pages. This bunny is not a replica of that Filler Bunny, but rather more of a nod to the idea. Creepy Filler Bunny is lots of fun to make, and a great knit whenever you're in a hurry and need to make something fast. Don't let his creepy demeanor fool you—he just needs cuddles like any other bunny!

INSTRUCTIONS

BODY

CO 6 sts, pm, and join.

Rnd 1: Kf&b in each st—12 sts.

Rnd 2: Knit around.

Rnd 3: Kf&b in each st—24 sts.

Rnd 4: Knit around.

Rnd 5: (K1, kf&b) around—36 sts.

Rnd 6: Knit around.

Rnd 7: (K2, kf&b) around—48 sts.

Rnd 8: K8, sl 6 sts to holder, k5, sl 6 sts to holder, knit to end.

Knit around on 36 sts for 3" (8 cm).

DECREASE ROWS

Rnd 1: (K6, k2tog) to last 4 sts, k4—32 sts.

Rnd 2: Knit.

Rnd 3: (K3, k2tog) to last 2 sts, k2—26 sts.

Rnd 4: Knit.

Rnd 5: (K3, k2tog) to last st, k1—21 sts.

Rnd 6: Knit.

Note: At this point, you may want to begin stuffing your bunny.

Rnd 7: (K2, k2tog)—14 sts.

Rnd 8: Knit around.

(K2tog) around—7 sts.

(K2tog) around until 6 sts remain.

Cut yarn leaving a 6" (15 cm) tail and pull through remaining sts to close.

FEET

Sl 6 sts for one foot from holder onto working needle.

Pick up and k6 sts from body of bunny, pm, and join.

Knit 4 rnds on 12 sts.

Fill foot with stuffing.

(K2tog) around to last 3 sts.

Cut tail and pull through remaining sts.

EARS (MAKE_2)

Count 5 rows down from top of bunny head.

Pick up 10 sts, then turn and pick up another 10 sts directly behind first set of 10. This separates your ears into front of bunny ear and back of bunny ear.

Knit around, for 22 rnds.

Next rnd (front of bunny ear): K2tog, k6, ssk. For back of bunny ear: k2tog, k6, ssk.

Next rnd: Knit for both front and back of bunny ear.

Repeat these 2 rnds until 2 sts remain, k2tog. Cut tail and pull through.

FINISHING

I lightly felted the bunny (page 125) to ensure the stuffing does not show through. However, it is not necessary.

Use the photo as a guide to sew on two buttons for eyes—one small and one large—to give your bunny an extra-creepy feel!

SKILL LEVEL
Easy

FINISHED MEASUREMENT
23" (58 cm)
circumference

MATERIALS
Lion Brand Jiffy (100%
acrylic; 3 oz/85g;
135 yd/123m): 2 skeins
in #196 Magenta

Size 10.5 (6.5 mm) 16"
(41 cm) circular needle

Size 10.5 (6.5 mm)
straight needles

Stitch markers

GAUGE
11 stitches and 16
rows = 4" (10 cm) in
Stockinette stitch on
size 10.5 (6.5 mm)
needles

CAT WOMAN HAT

: DESIGNED BY CALLIE NEED

This pattern was inspired by—who else?—Cat Woman! More cute than scary, this pattern is a fun, quick knit, a great stash buster, and perfect for gift giving! Make it unique by adding some stripes or intarsia! The best part? This is a project where you actually WANT to use cheaper, acrylic yarn! Because acrylic yarn is stiffer, it helps the hat hold its shape.

INSTRUCTIONS

With circular needle and two strands of yarn held together, CO 54 sts. Pm and join in the round.

Knit in the round until piece measures 7" (18 cm).

At the beginning of the next rnd, turn work inside out so WS is facing.

With straight needles, divide sts so that there are 27 sts on each needle.

Hold needles side by side and use the circular as your third needle, then make a three-needle bind off. Flip again so that the right side is now facing out.

Squared edges are now your "cat ears."

FLAPS (MAKE 2)

Using straight needles, pick up 9 sts from the brim under the squared edge on top.

Work St st for 4 rows.

Row 5: K1, k2tog, k3, k2tog, k1–7 sts.

Row 6: Purl.

Row 7: Knit.

Row 8: Purl.

Row 9: K1, k2tog, k1, k2tog, k1–5 sts.

Row 10: Purl.

Row 11: Knit.

Row 12: Purl.

Row 13: K2tog, k1, k2tog–3 sts.

Row 14: Purl. BO.

Make a flap for opposite side.

Weave in all ends.

HEY! FYI!

Did you know Leonard Nimoy has worked as a singer as well as an actor? His classic song "Ballad of Bilbo Baggins" with an accompanying video was released in the late 1960s!

SKILL LEVEL
Intermediate

SIZES
Small (medium, large)

FINISHED MEASUREMENTS
Tube top bust: 32 (36¾, 40½)" [81 (93, 103) cm]

Tube top length: 18" (46 cm)

Shrug length: 54" (137 cm)

MATERIALS
Stitch Nation Full 0' Sheep (100% Peruvian wool; 3.5 oz/100 g; 155 yd/142 m): 4 skeins in #2550 Plummy

Size 8 (5 mm) straight needles

Ten ½"/1 cm diameter buttons, in the color of your choice (I used pearl) [Note: You'll need 2 more buttons if you make the optional halter strap.]

Two safety pin—style stitch markers

GAUGE
17 stitches and 25 rows = 4" (10 cm) in Stockinette stitch on size 8 (5 mm) needles

MYSTIQUE

: DESIGNED BY TONI CARR

What's better than changing things up when you're bored? With this pattern, inspired of course by the beautiful shape-changing comic book character, you can easily swap from a shoulder-hugging sweater, just a tube top, a halter top, or a shrug!

Knit in three separate pieces, with only a little seaming required on the shrug, this piece is perfect for those nights out when you just can't make up your mind on what to wear. Change your look three times in one night!

INSTRUCTIONS

Note: Shrug is worked from side to side.

SHRUG

FIRST_SLEEVE

Beginning at the sleeve cuff, CO 32 (36, 40) sts.

Rows 1–8: K2, p2 rib.

Row 9: Knit.

Row 10: Purl.

Row 11: Knit.

Row 12: Purl.

Row 13: K1, M1, knit to last st, M1, k1—34 (38, 42) sts.

Row 14: Purl.

Row 15: Knit.

Row 16: Purl.

Repeat Rows 13–16 until there are 44 (48, 52) sts.

Work in St st for a total of 20 (21¼, 22)" [51 (54, 56) cm] from CO edge ending with a knit row.

Place stitch marker at each end of last row.

BACK

Row 1: K2, purl to last 2 sts, k2.

Row 2: Knit.

Repeat Rows 1 and 2 for 2" (5 cm) from markers, ending with Row 1.

Buttonhole Row 1 (RS): Knit to last 2 sts, BO 1.

Buttonhole Row 2: K1, CO 1, purl to last 2 sts, k2.

Repeat Rows 1 and 2 for 4" (4 ½, 5)" [10 (11, 13) cm], then repeat Buttonhole Rows 1 and 2.

Repeat entire section (starting with Row 1) once more for a total of 4 buttonholes.

SECOND_SLEEVE

Work in St st for an additional 16 (16¼, 16¾)" [41 (41, 43) cm] from last buttonhole, ending on a purl row.

Row 1 (RS): K1, k2tog, knit to last 3 sts, k2tog, k1.

Row 2: Purl.

Row 3: Knit.

Row 4: Purl.

Repeat Rows 1–4 until 32 (36, 40) sts remain.

Work in (k2,p2) rib for 8 rows.

BO in pattern.

FINISHING

Seam sleeves up to 2" (5 cm) away from first buttonhole.

TUBE TOP

CO 136 (156, 172) sts.

Row 1 (RS): (K2, p2) across.

Row 2 (WS): (P2, k2) across.

Repeat Rows 1 and 2 for 2" (5 cm) from beginning, ending WS.

Buttonhole Row 1: (K2, p2) to last 2 sts, BO 1.

Buttonhole Row 2: P1, CO 1, (k2, p2) across.

Work (k2, p2) rib for an additional 2" (5 cm) from buttonhole.

Next row: Knit to last 2 sts, BO 1.

Next row: P1, CO 1, purl to last end.

Next row: Knit across.

Next row: Purl across.

Repeat the last 2 rows for 2" (5 cm).

Note: Make sure to maintain buttonhole bind off on the same side of work each time.

Work Buttonhole Rows 1 and 2.

Repeat entire sequence until 8 buttonhole rows worked.

Work in (k2, p2) rib for next 8 rows.

BO in pattern.

FINISHING

On back of work, sew buttons to top ridge, lining up with buttonholes on shrug.

HALTER STRAP

If you want another fun twist on this top, add a halter strap to the tube top!

On the front of the tube top, sew two buttons on inside edge of top rib, wherever you would like halter straps to attach.

TO MAKE THE STRAP:

CO 6 sts.

Row 1: Knit.

Row 2: K3, BO 1, knit to end.

Row 3: K2, CO1, knit to end.

Work in g st for 22" (56 cm).

Next row: K3, BO 1, knit to end.

Next row: K2, CO 1, knit to end.

Next row: Knit.

BO.

OTHER STUFF FOR NERDS

: SKILL LEVEL

Intermediate

: FINISHED MEASUREMENTS

Kindle size: 6 x 8¼"
(15 x 23 cm)

iPad size: 7½ x 9.3"
(19 x 24 cm)

: MATERIALS

Plymouth Encore Worsted
(75% acrylic, 25% wool;
100g/200 yd): 1 skein

each in #1014 yellow
(MC) and #999 scarlet
(CC)

One 1" (3 cm) diameter
button

Size 9 (5.5 mm) straight
needles

Size G (4.25 mm) crochet
hook, for picking up
stitches if necessary

Sewing needle and thread

: GAUGE

24 stitches = 4" (9 cm)
in Linen stitch on size
9 (5.5 mm) needles

BOOK WIZARD

: DESIGNED BY GENEVIEVE MILLER

Most nerds are either big readers or big tech lovers. And lots are both! With all the great e-reader options available, many nerds are getting the best of both worlds. These expensive toys can be pretty delicate, however, so they need to be kept safe. With the Book Wizard, you can carry around your iPad or e-reader with a handy strap! This pattern is inspired by the thought of Hermione Granger lugging around her Hogwarts books until her bags literally burst at the seams. These are knit in Gryffindor colors, but can easily be changed for those Slytherins who want to fill their e-readers up with books from the forbidden section of the library!

SPECIAL INSTRUCTIONS

LINEN STITCH

All odd rows (RS): *K1, yf, s1 1 k-wise, yb; repeat from * across.

All even rows (WS): *P1, yb, s1 1 p-wise, yf; repeat from * across.

IPAD CASE INSTRUCTIONS

CO 56.

Work in Linen stitch with CC for 2" (5 cm), change to MC and work for 11" (28 cm). Change back to CC for 1" (3 cm) more before Top Flap Shaping, ending WS.

KINDLE CASE INSTRUCTIONS

CO 50 sts.

Work in Linen stitch in CC for 2" (5 cm), change to MC and work for 9" (23 cm). Change back to CC for 1½" (4 cm) more before Top Flap Shaping.

TOP FLAP SHAPING (FOR BOTH CASES)

Row 1 (RS): Ssk; *k1, yf, sl 1 k-wise, yb; repeat from * across, ending k2tog—54 sts.

Row 2: Ssp, *p1, yb, s1 p-wise, yf; repeat from * across, ending p2tog—52 sts.

Repeat last 2 rows until 20 sts remain, ending RS.

BUTTONHOLE (FOR BOTH CASES)

With the remaining 20 sts, follow the pattern across first 7 sts, BO 5 sts as follows:

yf, sl 1 p-wise, yb, sl 1 p-wise, psso (yf, sl 1 p-wise, yb, psso, yb, sl 1 p-wise, psso) twice

(yb, sl 1 p-wise, yf, p1) across, ending yb, sl 1 p-wise.

Next row (RS): Follow pattern across 8 sts, CO 5, pattern to end.

Rows 1–6: Continue established pattern.

BO in pattern.

FINISHING

Weave in ends. With WS facing you, fold so that the first row is even with the last row before decreases. Seam sides together with appropriate yarn color. Turn inside out so that RS is facing out. With the flap down, mark where the button will go and sew on the button.

STRAP (OPTIONAL)

CO 12 sts in either color. Repeat in pattern for 42" (107 cm) or desired length. Weave in ends. Sew onto each side of the top of the case.

SKILL LEVEL
Easy

FINISHED MEASUREMENTS
60" (152 cm) long by 4" (10 cm) wide at the widest portion

MATERIALS
Knit Picks Swish DK (100% superwash Merino wool; 50g/123 yd): 1 skein each in #24633 Bark (Color A) and #24314 Persimmon Heather (Color B)

Size 5 (3.75 mm) straight needles

GAUGE
24 stitches and 30 rows = 4" (10 cm) in Stockinette stitch on size 5 (3.75 mm) needles

TIE IT ON

: DESIGNED BY TONI CARR

This is a great pattern for the newer knitter ready to try a little bit of charting! This tie whips up quickly and is a great way to show a little bit of nerd pride!

INSTRUCTIONS

With Color A, CO 2 sts.

Row 1 (RS): (Kf&b) twice—4 sts.

Row 2: K1, purl to last st, k1.

Row 3: K1, (kf&b) twice, k1—6 sts.

Row 4: K1, purl to last st, k1.

Row 5: K1, kf&b, knit to last 2 sts, kf&b, k1—8 sts.

Row 6: K1, purl to last st, k1.

Row 7: Continue increases on every RS row until 22 sts are on the needle.

Next row: K1, purl to last st, k1.

Next row: K11, kf&b, k10—23 sts.

Next row: K1, purl to last st, k1.

Continue in St st (knitting first and last st on purl rows) and begin DNA Chart Pattern, working until tie measures 6" (15 cm) from beginning.

TIE_SHAPING

Begin decreases (while still working DNA pattern).

Row 1 (RS): K1, k2tog, knit to last 3 sts, k2tog, k1—21 sts.

Row 2: K1, purl to last st, k1.

Row 3: Knit.

Row 4: K1, purl to last st, k1.

Row 5: K1, k2tog to last 3 sts, k2tog, k1—
19 sts.

Work in St st (and DNA Chart Pattern) until tie
measures 17" (43 cm) from beginning, ending
on WS.

Next row: Slip as if to purl, k2tog, knit to last
3 sts, ssk, k1.

Next row: Knit.

Repeat last 2 rows until 7 sts remain.

Continue in St st until tie measures 60"
(152 cm).

BO.

FINISHING

Weave in all ends and block (page 122).

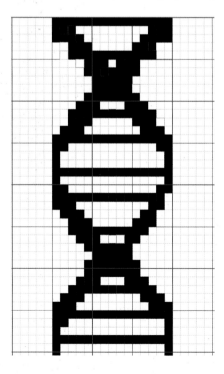

: SKILL LEVEL

Advanced

: SIZES

Small (medium, large)

: FINISHED MEASUREMENTS

Chest: 37 (42½, 45)"
[94 (108, 114) cm]

Length: 28¾ (30, 30¾)"
[73 (76, 78) cm]

: MATERIALS

Lion Brand Wool Ease
(80% acrylic, 20% wool;
3 oz/85g, 197 yd/180m):
4 skeins in #620-152
Oxford Grey

Size 7 (4.5 mm) straight
needles

Size 9 (5.5 mm) straight
needles

Size 7 (4.5 mm) 16"
(41 cm) circular needle

Cable needle (CN)

Stitch markers

Stitch holder

: GAUGE

20 stitches and 24
rows = 4" (10 cm) in
Stockinette stitch on
size 9 (5.5 mm) needles

BIG BANG GUY'S SWEATER VEST

: DESIGNED BY TONI CARR AND IRENE BASEY

The guy's version of this is inspired by the character Raj on *The Big Bang Theory* television show. This is based on the pattern my grandmother designed, knit, and always crammed over my brother's head!

The cable pattern adds a lot of texture to the vest, making it extra chunky and perfect for studying late in a drafty library or running around campus!

CABLE_PATTERN

Notes: C6B: Slip 3 sts to CN and hold at back, k3, k3 sts from CN. Stitches between [brackets] indicate number of stitches for various sizes.

Rows 1 and 3 (RS): K1, p1, [k1 (k2, k2)], p1; *k6, [p1 (p2, p2)], k2, [p1 (p1, p2)], k2, [p1 (p2, p2)]; repeat from * across, ending k6, p1, [k1 (k2, k2)], p1, k1.

Rows 2 and 4: P1, k1, [p1 (p2, p2)], k1, p6; * [k1 (k2, k2)], p2, [k1 (k1, k2)], p2, [k1 (k2, k2)], p6; repeat from * across, ending k1, [p1 (p2, p2)], k1, p1.

Row 5: K1, p1, [k1 (k2, k2)], p1; * C6B, [p1 (p2, p2)], k2, [p1 (p1, p2)], k2, [p1 (p2, p2)]; repeat from * across, ending C6B, p1, [k1 (k2, k2)], p1, k1.

Rows 6 and 8: Repeat Row 2.

Rows 7 and 9: Repeat Row 1.

Row 10: Repeat Row 5.

INSTRUCTIONS

BACK

With smaller straight needles, CO 92 (104, 112) sts.

Work in (k2, p2) rib for 2½" (6 cm), ending WS and increasing 0 (1, 0) st each edge—92 (106, 112) sts.

With larger needles, work Cable Pattern until piece measures 19 (19½, 20)" [48 (50, 51) cm].

ARMHOLE SHAPING

Keeping to Cable Pattern as best you can, at beg of each of the next 4 rows, BO 2 (5, 5) sts—84 (16, 92) sts.

Decrease 1 st each edge, EOR 2 (3, 3) times—80 (80, 86) sts.

Work even until armhole measures 9 (9¾, 10)" [23 (24, 25) cm].

At beg of each of the next 10 (10, 8) rows, BO 5 (5, 7) sts—30 (30, 30) sts.

Place remaining sts on holder.

FRONT

Work same as back to armhole until there are 80 (80, 86) sts, ending WS.

NECK SHAPING

Next row: Work (k2, p2) rib for 40 (40, 43) sts, join another ball of yarn, work (k2, p2) rib for remaining sts. Working sides separately and at the same time, dec 1 st each neck edge every 4 rows 8 (10, 12) times—32 (30, 31) sts remain for each shoulder.

Decrease 1 st each neck edge EOR 7 (5, 3) times—25 (25, 28) sts remain for each shoulder.

Continue in pattern until armhole measures 9 (9¾, 10)" [23 (24, 25) cm].

At each arm edge, BO 5 (5, 7) sts 5 (5, 4) times.

FINISHING

Sew side and shoulder seams.

ARMBANDS

Using circular needle with RS facing, pick up 112 (116, 120) sts around armhole.

(K2, p2) rib for 1" (3 cm).

BO in rib pattern.

Repeat for other armhole.

NECKBAND

With RS facing and circular needle, pick up 30 (30, 30) sts from holder, pm, pick up 57 (61, 61) sts from left front, pm, pick up 57 (61, 61) sts from right front, pm, join—144 (152, 152) sts.

Row 1: (K2, p2) rib to last 3 sts before second marker, k3, sm, k3, (p2, k2) rib to last marker, ending p2.

Row 2: (K2, p2) rib to last 3 sts before second marker, k2tog, k1, sm, k1, sl 1, k1, psso, (k2, p2) rib to last marker—142 (150, 150) sts.

Row 3: Work in established rib pattern.

Repeat Rows 2 and 3 for 1" (3 cm).

BO in rib.

QUESTION:

If you were transported hundreds of years into the future, almost everyone spoke Chinese, and good things were described as "shiny," what color coat should you wear?

A. A red coat
B. A blue coat
C. A brown coat

Answer: C. You would be in the world of the television show *Firefly.* You would want to wear a brown coat and you would aim to misbehave!

SKILL LEVEL

Intermediate

SIZE

Women's extra-small
(small, medium, large)

FINISHED MEASUREMENTS

Finished bust: 30 (36,
40, 46)" [76 (91, 102,
117) cm]

Finished length: 24 (24,
24½, 25)" [61 (61, 62,
64) cm]

MATERIALS

Lion Brand Wool Ease
(80% acrylic, 20% wool;
3 oz/85 g, 197 yd/
180 m): 2 (2, 3, 3)
skeins in #157 Pastel
Yellow or #104 Blush
Heather (Model shown in
Blush Heather)

Size 5 (3.75 mm)
straight needles

Size 7 (4.5 mm) straight
needles

Size 5 (3.75 mm) 16"
(41 cm) circular needle

Two stitch markers

Tapestry needle

GAUGE

16 stitches and 22
rows = 4" (10 cm) in
Stockinette stitch on
size 7 (4.5 mm) needles

BIG BANG GIRL'S SWEATER VEST

: DESIGNED BY TONI CARR AND IRENE BASEY

This vest is based on the work uniform of the sexy next-door neighbor on *The Big Bang Theory*, Penny. Worked flat with ribbing added around the neck and sleeves after seaming, it knits up in a flash and is the perfect finishing touch to your Penny and Leonard costumes for Halloween, or the next Comic-Con.

INSTRUCTIONS

BACK

With smaller straight needles, CO 60 (72, 80, 92) sts.

Work (k1, p1) rib for 1" (3 cm).

Change to larger needles and work in St st until piece measures 15 (15, 16, 17)" [38 (38, 41, 43) cm] from beginning.

ARMHOLE SHAPING

BO 2 (4, 4, 6) sts at beg of next 2 rows—56 (64, 72, 80) sts.

BO 2 (3, 4, 4) sts at beg of next 2 rows—52 (58, 64, 72) sts.

BO 2 (3, 3, 5) sts at beg of next 2 rows—48, (52, 58, 62) sts.

Continue in St st until piece measures 23 (23, 24½, 25¾)" [58 (58, 62, 65) cm] ending with a WS row.

BO 4 (3, 4, 4) sts at beg of next 2 rows—40 (46, 50, 54) sts.

BO 2 (3, 3, 4) sts at beg of next 2 rows—36 (40, 44, 46) sts.

BO remaining sts.

FRONT

Work same as for back until piece measures 12½" (32 cm) from beginning, ending with a WS row.

NECK SHAPING

K28 (34, 38, 44), k2tog, join new ball of yarn, k2tog, knit to end—29 (35, 39, 45) sts each edge.

Working sides separately but at same time, decrease 1 st each neck edge every row 17 (19, 21, 23) times. AT THE SAME TIME: when piece measures 15" (38 cm) from beginning, begin armhole shaping.

ARMHOLE SHAPING

1st Armhole Row: BO 2 (4, 4, 6) sts at each armhole edge.

Next row: BO 2 (3, 4, 4) sts at each armhole edge.

Next row: BO 2 (3, 3, 5) sts at each armhole edge.

Continue in St st until piece measures 23 (23, 24½, 25¾)" [58 (58, 62, 65) cm] from beginning, ending on a WS row.

Next row: BO 4 (3, 4, 4) sts at each armhole edge—8 (10, 11, 12) sts remain for each shoulder.

Next rows: BO 2 (3, 3, 4) sts at beg of next two rows.

BO remaining sts.

FINISHING

Sew shoulder and side seams.

NECKBAND

With RS facing, using circular needle and beginning at left shoulder, pick up and k56 (56, 58, 58) sts along left front, pm, pick up 2 sts from center.

Pm, pick up and k56 (56, 58, 58) sts along right front neck edge, then pick up and k35 (39, 43, 45) sts along back neck—149 (153, 161, 163) sts.

Rnd 1: (K1, p1) to marker, sm, k2, sm, p1, k1, ending p1.

Rnd 2: (K1, p1) rib to last 2 sts before marker, k2tog, sm, k2, sm, k2tog, rib to end—147 (151, 159, 161) sts.

Rnd 3: (K1, p1) rib to first marker, sm, k2tog, sm, rib to end—146 (150, 158, 160) sts.

Rnd 4: (K1, p1) rib to last 2 sts before marker, p2tog, sm, k1, sm, p2tog, rib to end—144 (148, 156, 158) sts.

Rnd 5: (K1, p1) rib to marker, sm, k1, sm, rib to end.

BO in pattern.

ARMBANDS

With RS facing, using circular needle, beginning at side seams, pick up and k96 (96, 102, 108) sts around armhole edge. Pm and work 1 x 1 rib around for 5 rounds.

BO in pattern.

SKILL LEVEL

Intermediate

SIZE

Women's size small (medium, large, extra-large)

FINISHED MEASUREMENTS

Bust: 45 (47, 49, 51)" [114 (119, 124, 130) cm]

Length: 39 (41, 41½, 43½)" [99 (104, 105, 110) cm]

MATERIALS

Knit Picks Swish Bulky (100% superwash Merino wool; 100 g/137 yd): 8 (8, 9, 10) skeins in #24367 Blackberry

Size 10.5 (6.5 mm) 29" (74 cm) circular needle

Stitch holder

Yarn needle

GAUGE

15 stitches and 21 rows = 4" (10 cm) in Stockinette stitch on size 10.5 (6.5 mm) needles

REAL GENIUS SWEATER

DESIGNED BY TONI CARR

One of my favorite '80s movies is called *Real Genius*. The best part of the movie for me wasn't the super laser, the 15-year-old genius, or even the secret tunnels! It was Mitch Taylor being presented with a sweater handknit for him overnight by the always-awake Jordan.

This off-the-shoulder tunic is an homage to that scene. While it's knit in bulky yarn, you may not be able to whip it up in a single night (unless, of course, you never sleep) but you could easily make it in a single weekend. It's the perfect project for procrastinating on that final paper!

INSTRUCTIONS

BACK

CO 72 (76, 80, 84) sts.

Work (k1, p1) rib for 3½ (3¾, 4, 4)" [9 (10, 10, 10) cm].

Beginning with a knit row, work in St st for 10 (10, 14, 14) rows, ending with a purl row.

Row 1 (RS): Continue in St st, increase 1 st at beg and end of row—2 sts added.

Rows 2–8: Continue in St st.

Repeat Rows 1–8 for 5 more times—84 (88, 92, 96).

Work in St st until back measures 26 (28, 28, 30)" [66 (71, 71, 76) cm] from beg, ending with a WS row.

RAGLAN SHAPING

For all sizes, BO 2 sts at beg of next 2 rows—80 (84, 88, 92) sts.

Row 1 (RS): K1, k2tog, knit to last 2 sts, sl 1, k1, psso, k1.

Row 2: Purl.

Row 3: Knit.

Row 4: Purl.

Repeat Rows 1-4 for 2 more times—74 (78, 82, 86) sts.

*Next row: K1, k2tog, knit to last 3 sts, sl 1, k1, psso, k1—2 sts decreased.

Next row: Purl. **

Repeat last 2 rows until 56 (60, 64, 68) sts remain, ending WS; place sts on holder.

FRONT

Work same as Back to **.

Repeat from * to ** until there are 64 (68, 72, 76) sts remaining.

NECK

LEFT SIDE

Row 1 (RS): K1, k2tog , k8—10 sts. Place remaining 53 (57, 61, 65) sts on holder.

Row 2: Purl.

Row 3: K1, k2tog, knit to last 3 sts, sl 1, k1, psso, k1—8 sts.

Row 4: Purl.

Row 5: K1, k2tog, knit to last 3 sts, sl 1, k1, psso, k1—6 sts.

Row 6: Purl.

Row 7: K1, k2tog, knit to end—5 sts.

Row 8: Purl.

Row 9: K1, k2tog, knit to end—4 sts.

Row 10: Purl.

Row 11: K1, k2tog knit to end—3 sts.

Row 12: Purl.

Row 13: K1, k2tog—2 sts.

Row 14: P2tog.

BO.

RIGHT SIDE

With RS facing, sl next 42 (46, 50, 54) sts onto st holder. Join yarn to remaining 11 sts.

Row 1 (RS): Knit to last 3 sts, sl 1, k1, psso, k1—10 sts.

Row 2: Purl.

Row 3: K1, k2tog, knit to last 3 sts, sl 1, k1, psso, k1—8 sts.

Row 4: Purl.

Row 5: K1, k2tog, knit to last 3 sts, sl 1, k1, psso, k1—6 sts.

Row 6: Purl.

Row 7: Knit to last 3 sts, sl 1, k1, psso, k1—5 sts.

Row 8: Purl.

Row 9: Knit to last 3 sts, sl 1, k1, psso, k1—4 sts.

Row 10: Purl.

Row 11: K1, k2tog, k1—3 sts.

Row 12: Purl.

Row 13: K1, k2tog—2 sts.

Row 14: P2tog.

BO.

SLEEVES (MAKE_2)

CO 48 (48, 52, 52) sts.

Work (k1, p1) rib for 6 (6, 8, 8) rows.

Beginning with a knit row, work St st for 8 (8, 10, 10) rows.

RAGLAN SHAPING

BO 2 sts at the beg of next 2 rows—44 (44, 48, 48) sts.

Row 1 (RS): K1, k2tog, knit to last 3 sts, sl 1, k1, psso, k1—2 sts decreased.

Row 2: Purl.

Repeat Rows 1 and 2 until there are 22 (22, 26, 26) sts, ending WS. Work 2 rows even in (k1, p1) rib. Place sts on holder. Make second sleeve.

NECK BAND

Note: To make working the neck easier, try seaming the sides before you begin working in the round.

With RS facing, k22 (22, 26, 26) sleeve sts, decreasing 1 st each edge—20 (20, 24, 24) sts.

Pick up 12 sts along neck edge, k42 (46, 50, 54) sts from front neck holder, pick up 12 sts along neck edge, knit sts from right sleeve holder, decreasing 1 st from each edge—20 (20, 24, 24) sts. Knit across 56 (60, 64, 68) back sts, pm to join in the round.

Knit 4 rnds on 162 (170, 186, 194) sts.

Next rnd: Decrease 10 sts evenly over sleeve, 18 sts evenly over front, 10 sts evenly over next sleeve, and 16 sts from back—108 (116, 132, 140) sts.

Work (k1, p1) rib for 3½ (3½, 4, 4)" [9 (9, 10, 10) cm].

BO in rib.

Seam sides and sleeves.

: SKILL LEVEL

Intermediate

: FINISHED MEASUREMENTS

18½" (47 cm) wide and
13½" (34 cm) tall after
felting

: MATERIALS

Knit Picks Wool of the
Andes Worsted (100%
Peruvian highland wool;
50 g /110 yd): 4 skeins
in #23420 Coal (Color A)
and 2 skeins in #24065
White (Color B)

Bag strap (available
at any craft store) or
guitar strap (available
from any filk musician)

Buttons for attaching
the guitar strap
(optional)

Size 8 (5 mm) straight
needles

Size 8 (5 mm) 29"
(74 cm) circular needle

Tapestry needle

Sewing needle and thread

: GAUGE

20 stitches and 20
rows = 4" (10 cm) in
Stockinette stitch on
size 8 (5 mm) needles

CHECKMATE! LAPTOP BAG

: DESIGNED BY TONI CARR

What's more perfect for the nerd on the go
than a laptop bag that not only can haul your
computer around, but can also be used to
challenge your friends to a game of chess?
That's multitasking!

This bag is felted so that it's extremely
durable. But if you choose not to felt the bag,
make sure you line it with fabric so that it
doesn't stretch out when you put your laptop
and books inside it.

INSTRUCTIONS

With Color A, CO 104 sts.

Knit 9 rows in g st, noting first row as WS.

*Note: The chessboard is worked in St st using two colors.
When changing colors, bring next strand from under present
strand for a twist to prevent holes. Carry unused strand
loosely along WS, twisting every 3 to 4 sts.*

Row 1 (RS): With Color A, k4; *k12-Color B, k12-Color A;
repeat from * across, ending k4-Color A.

Keeping 4 sts at each edge in g st in Color A, work 1 white
and 1 black square across for 4 times. Alternate squares,
with 8 squares across and 8 squares down. Cut Color B.

With Color A, work in St st for 15" (38 cm) to equal length of
chart pattern. Knit 9 rows Color A in g st. BO loosely.

FINISHING

Use a needle and thread to sew up the sides, leaving the top open.

You can felt the bag (page 125), or if you would like your bag large, line it with fabric.

Sew the strap to each side securely at the top. I always sew a button on each side and use an old guitar strap!

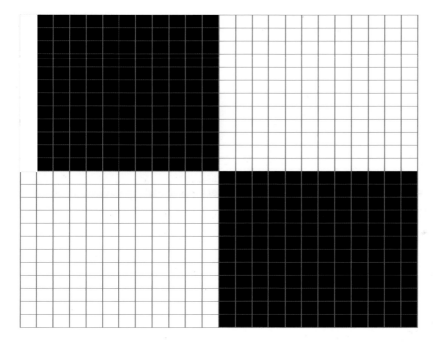

QUESTION:

You're walking around and notice an angel statue holding its hands over its eyes. What should you do?

    A. Stare at it and back slowly away, never taking your eyes off of it.

    B. Take a nap at the angel's feet. Looks comfy!

    C. Find the nearest blue police box!

Answer: Both A and C are correct. You've just encountered a weeping angel from *Doctor Who*. They can only get you if you blink or turn away. So don't blink! And find the blue police box with the Doctor as quickly as possible. He'll know what to do!

: SKILL LEVEL
Easy

: FINISHED MEASUREMENTS
23½" (67 cm) around and 6" (15 cm) wide

: MATERIALS
Knit Picks Swish Worsted (100% superwash Merino wool; 50 g/110 yd): 1 skein in #24310 Amethyst Heather

Size 8 (5 mm) 16" (41 cm) circular needle, or 29" (74 cm) circular needle for the scarf variation

Stitch marker

: GAUGE
19 stitches and 25 rows= 4" (10 cm) in garter stitch on size 8 (5 mm) needles

: SPECIAL INSTRUCTIONS
Creating the twist is done when joining in the round. Simply line up your stitches as you would for normal circular knitting, but at the join, twist the last stitch around, then join.

MÖBIUS

: DESIGNED BY TONI CARR

This is a fun project for the math nerd! The Möbius was discovered by German mathematicians August Ferdinand Möbius and Johann Benedict Listing in the mid-1800s. A Möbius has only one side and one boundary component. It's not only a nerdy knit for math lovers, it's also fun to make, since you get to do something you're never, ever supposed to do when knitting—twist in the round!

This pattern is just for a basic neck warmer Möbius with some additional instructions on how to make a longer scarf. It's also easy to knit a large möbius to make a shoulder shrug. An infinite loop means infinite possibilities!

INSTRUCTIONS

CO 118 sts, pm, and join with a twist.

You will now be knitting in the round, with your stitches twisted once to create a cool infinite loop.

Rnd 1: Knit.

Rnd 2: Purl.

Repeat Rnds 1 and 2 for 6" (15 cm).

BO loosely.

LONGER_SCARF

[52¾" (134 cm) around and 4" (10 cm) wide]:

CO 250 sts, pm, and join with a twist.

Work in g st for 4" (10 cm).

BO loosely.

Note: Wrap the scarf twice around your neck for a double loop.

: KNITTING ABBREVIATIONS AND TECHNIQUES

ABBREVIATIONS

beg = beginning

BO = bind off

CC = contrasting color

ch = crochet chain

CO = cast on

dec = decrease

DK = double knitting weight yarn

DPN(s) = double-pointed needle(s)

EOR = end of row

g st = garter stitch

inc = increase

k = knit

k2tog = knit 2 stitches together

k3tog = knit 3 stitches together

kf&b = knit 1 stitch in front, then in back

k-wise = knit-wise, as if being knit

M1 = make 1 stitch

MC = main color

p = purl

p2tog = purl 2 stitches together

pm = place marker

psso = pass next stitch over

p-wise = purl-wise, as if being purled

rnd = round

RS = right side

sc = single crochet

sl = slip a stitch

sm = slip marker

ssk = slip, slip, knit decrease

st(s) = stitch(es)

St st = Stockinette stitch

tog = together

w&t = wrap and turn

WS = wrong side

yb = yarn in back

yf = yarn in front

yo = yarn over (wrap yarn around right needle)

TECHNIQUES

BAR INCREASE OR MAKE ONE (M1)

Note: The bar increase is sometimes listed in a pattern as M1, for make 1.

1. Insert the tip of the right needle under the horizontal bar that runs between the two stitches on your needles.

2. Slip the bar onto the left needle and knit through the back loop. This creates a brand-new stitch from between the previous two stitches.

BIND OFF (BO)

Here are a couple different ways: Basic Bind Off and Three-Needle Bind Off.

Basic Bind Off

1. Knit one stitch.

2. Knit another stitch.

3. Pass the first knit stitch over the second. (My grandmother used to tell me to visualize playing leap frog!)

4. Repeat Steps 2 and 3 until all stitches are off the needle.

Three-Needle Bind Off

This is a great bind off that seams and binds off your finished work at the same time.

1. With both RS facing, insert the tip of a third needle into the first stitch of the right-hand needle, then into the first stitch of the left-hand needle.

2. Knit these two stitches together.

3. Knit the first stitch from each needle together. Pass the previous stitch over this stitch.

Repeat Step 3 until all stitches are off the needles.

BLOCKING

Blocking is the final step in your knitting. After felting, it helps determine the size and shape of your finished item. For other knit items, it smoothes out irregularities, can soften a stiff or coarse yarn, and can even allow you to reshape your item. Every yarn is different, so refer to the handling instructions on your yarn for blocking care and instructions.

STEAM BLOCKING

1. Lay out your knitting on a surface suitable for pressing, such as a blocking mat. Place WS up and pin into shape.

2. Steam the fabric by hovering a steam iron above the surface, but do not let the iron touch the knitting. Work in sections, saturating each section with steam before moving on to the next section. (*Note: Don't steam block any yarn that might not be colorfast. If in doubt, steam block your fabric swatch first.*)

3. Let dry.

WET BLOCKING

1. Soak your knitting in a sink full of lukewarm water until fully saturated.

2. Gently squeeze and press out as much water as possible, being careful not to wring or twist the fabric. Wrap the knitting in a bath towel and let it sit to absorb more water.

3. Lay the knitting out on a dry towel. Pin and shape as needed, then leave it out to dry completely. If the finished item is heavy, such as a sweater, it's best to flip the item over halfway through the drying process.

CABLE STITCH

The cable stitch is a fun, easy way to incorporate cool twists, textures, and patterns into your work. When you cable stitch, you are essentially crossing one stitch over the other. Each pattern will determine how many stitches your cable needs. For example: C6F translates to your finished cable being 6 stitches wide, and twisting by holding your cable needle in the front.

1. Slip 3 stitches to your cable needle, and hold in the front.

2. Knit the next 3 stitches from your left hand needle.

3. Knit the stitches from your cable needle. Combined with the rest of your pattern, this will give you a cable running through your work.

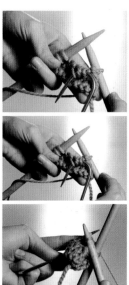

CAST ON (CO)

There are many ways to cast on! Here are the four that I use the most:

Long Tail Cast On

1. Make a slip knot in your yarn, leaving an appropriate length tail. (Hint: If you need to cast on 70 stitches, wrap your yarn 70 times around your needle, then make your slip knot. This gives you the correct tail length.). Insert the thumb and forefinger of your left hand between the strands of yarn with the working end around your forefinger and the tail end around your thumb. Lay your hand flat, so the yarn is flush with the palm of your hand.

2. Insert the tip of the right needle into the loop on your thumb, point the tip up, and pull down through the loop on your forefinger, then draw up a loop with the needle. Remove your thumb and pull the working yarn to tighten the stitch slightly on the needle.

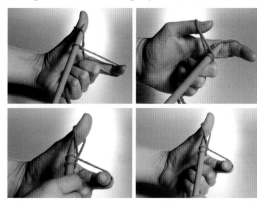

3. Repeat until you have the desired number of stitches on your right-hand needle.

Cable Cast On

1. Make a slip knot. Knit into your slip knot, leaving the stitch on the left-hand needle. Place the new stitch onto the left needle by slipping it knit-wise.

2. Knit into the gap between the last two stitches on the left needle. Slip the knit stitch onto the left-hand needle by slipping it knit-wise.

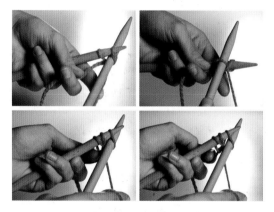

Provisional Cast On

This cast on leaves live stitches on your edge. It's perfect if you want to go back, pick up stitches on an edge, and continue knitting (such as in the Light of Eärendil Shrug on page 17). You will need your working yarn, as well as some waste yarn.

1. Make a slip knot with both the working yarn and the waste yarn, and place them on your needle.

2. With both working yarn and waste yarn, prepare for the long tail cast on. When setting up for your loops, put the working yarn around your index finger, and the waste yarn around your thumb.

3. Work your cast on as you normally would with the long tail cast on method. The waste yarn will form what looks like a crochet chain underneath your working yarn. If you end up with a waste yarn loop on your needle, pull it off! You've made a mistake and need to work that stitch again.

4. Begin working your stitches as called for in the pattern.

5. When it's time to work with these stitches again, very carefully unravel your waste yarn, and place them on your needle.

Backward Loop Cast On

Note: This is the perfect cast on for when you need to add stitches in the middle of a project, such as making a buttonhole.

1. Wrap the working yarn counterclockwise around your left thumb.

2. Insert the right hand needle into the loop on your thumb. Remove your thumb and pull the yarn to tighten it onto the needle (but not too tightly!). Repeat the last two steps until you have the required number of stitches cast onto your needle.

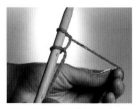

CROCHET CHAIN (ch)

1. Make a slip knot and place it on your crochet hook.

2. Bring your yarn over the hook, drawing the yarn over through the loop on the hook. Repeat until you achieve your desired number of stitches.

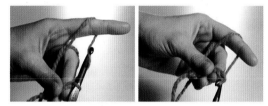

FELTING

Felting is fun and easy. You can felt with any animal fiber, but not cotton or acrylic. There are a couple of ways to do this.

Washing Machine Method:

Put your knit item into a fabric bag or zippered pillowcase. Set your washing machine on hot, and throw it in the machine with another item to help with the agitation. (I have a pair of old jeans I keep around specifically to felt with.) Check your item periodically to make sure it's not shrinking too much. If it comes out a little too small, don't worry! It can usually be stretched and blocked back to size.

Hand Felting:

Don't have a washing machine handy? You can still felt! In your bathtub or kitchen sink, soak the item in hot water with a little bit of dish soap. You'll want to agitate the item, but it's best to use a tool for that, since you don't want to burn your hands! I find that a small sink plunger works great. Once your knit item is the correct size, run it under cold water to rinse and block.

FRINGE ATTACHMENT

Fringe is fun and easy to make! You need a crochet hook, a piece of cardboard, and a pair of scissors.

Making Fringe

1. Cut your cardboard into a square in the size determined by your pattern. For example, if your pattern calls for 6-inch (15 cm) fringe, you want your cardboard to be a 6-inch (15 cm) square.

2. Wrap yarn around the cardboard to your desired fringe thickness.

3. Cut the all the strands of yarn on one side only of the cardboard.

Attaching Fringe

1. Use a crochet hook to pull the fringe through the edge of your fabric, in between stitches.

2. Line up the fringe so that the ends are even on both sides.

3. Tie a knot in the fringe at the fabric edge.

GARTER STITCH (g st)

The garter stitch is created simply by knitting every single row. Both the front and the back of the finished work will look the same.

I-CORD

Also called the "idiot cord" thanks to its creator Elizabeth Zimmerman, this knitting technique is the perfect example of a knitting mistake gone awesome! The I-cord is great for decorative edging or purse straps.

1. Cast on the number of stitches called for in the pattern onto one double pointed needle.

2. Knit those stitches; then instead of turning your work, slide the stitches to the end of the needle.

3. Place the needle in your left hand, and knit. It will feel a little awkward at first, since the yarn you are knitting is coming from the far side of the needle, instead of the side closest to you.

Repeat until the I-cord is the desired length.

KITCHENER STITCH

The Kitchener stitch is a great way to close an opening, such as the toe of a sock. Working in live stitches on your needles, you need an even number of stitches for this one to work!

1. Bring the yarn through the first front stitch purl-wise and leave the stitch on the tapestry needle.

2. Bring the yarn through the first back stitch knit-wise and leave the stitch on the needle.

3. Bring the yarn through the first front stitch knit-wise and slip the stitch off the needle.

4. Bring the yarn through the next front stitch purl-wise and leave the stitch on the needle.

5. Bring the yarn through the first back stitch purl-wise and slip the stitch off the needle.

6. Bring the yarn through the next back stitch knit-wise and leave the stitch on the needle.

Repeat Steps 3 through 6.

KNIT STITCH (K)

1. Place the needle with your cast on stitches in your left hand and your empty needle in your right hand.

2. Hold the working yarn to the back of your work. Slip the tip of your right-hand needle front to back, into the first loop on the left-hand needle.

3. With the needle in position, carry the working yarn over the right-hand needle, counterclockwise around the needle and in between both needles.

4. Slide the right-hand needle down, with the loop close to the tip of the needle (but don't let the loop fall off!). With the tip of the needle close to the edge of the left needle, push the right-hand needle in front of the left-hand needle.

5. Slide the right-hand needle up. Let the first loop on the left-hand needle slide off.

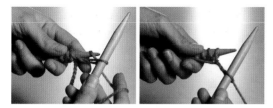

KNIT 2 TOGETHER DECREASE / PURL 2 TOGETHER (k2tog/p2tog)

Knit 2 Together

This is a really simple decrease that will slope to the right (as opposed to ssk, which will slope to the left). Simply knit two stitches together as one and you will have your k2tog decrease!

Purl 2 Together

As with k2tog, purl two stitches together as one for a right-sloping decrease.

KNIT FRONT AND BACK INCREASE (Kf&b)

1. Knit into the front of the stitch in the normal manner, then before removing the stitch from the needle, knit again into the back loop of the stitch.
2. Slip the stitch off the needle.

PASS SLIPPED STITCH OVER (psso)

1. Pass the slipped stitch onto the right-hand needle over the next stitch, as if to bind off.

PICKING UP STITCHES

On a horizontal edge, such as the top of a shoulder seam:

1. With RS facing, insert the right needle from front to back into the center of the first full stitch below the edge of the work.
2. Wrap the yarn around the needle and pull the loop through to create the new stitch.
3. Work Steps 1 and 2 for each stitch.

For a vertical edge:

1. With RS facing, insert the needle from front to back into the space between the first two stitches of your row.
2. Wrap the yarn around the needle and pull the loop through to create the new stitch.
3. Repeat Steps 1 and 2 for each stitch.

Hint: If you're having trouble with the stitches falling off the needle, try using a small crochet hook to pick up your stitches. Slide them onto your needle as you create each loop.

POM-POMS

1. To make a pom-pom, cut a 2-inch (5 cm) circle from a piece of cardboard. Cut a smaller circle in the center, about 1/2-inch (1 cm) in diameter. Your circle should look like a donut.
2. Thread your yarn through the hole in the circle, then wrap it around the outer circle over and over until you can't see cardboard at all. The yarn should be nice and thick! The thicker your yarn, the more your pom-pom will pop.

When finished, cut around the outer edge of the yarn, then tie the middle of the pom-pom with a 6-inch (15 cm) piece of yarn. Use the longer thread of yarn to tie the pom-pom to your fabric.

128

PURL STITCH (P)

1. Hold the working yarn to the front of your work and insert the needle from back to front though the first loop on the left-hand needle.

2. Bring the working yarn top to bottom over the right-hand needle.

3. Pull the loop on the right-hand needle out through the stitch on the left needle.

4. Slip the stitch off the left-hand needle.

RIB STITCH

The rib stitch alternates knitting and purling stitches. The rib stitch can work in many different combinations, such as a 1 x 1 rib, 2 x 2 rib, 3 x 3 rib, etc., as long as you always end on the purl stitches in your sequence. For example, in a 2 x 2 rib, you knit two stitches, then purl two stitches, and so on, ending on a purl 2. For each subsequent row, you use the same alternating pattern. The rib stitch creates a nice stretchy fabric

that is ribbed on both sides. It's perfect for hats, hems on sweaters, or anywhere you want a little stretch.

Seed Stitch:

Seed Stitch creates another stretchy fabric. It's easy to do, and it's created by alternating ribs and purls. For example:

Row 1: (Knit 1, p1) to end.

Row 2: (Purl 1, k1) to end.

Repeating those two rows will create the seed stitch!

SEAMING

There are lots of ways to seam, and depending on your finished item, some will look better than others.

Mattress Stitch:

The mattress stitch is best used for creating invisible seams in side-to-side Stockinette stitch. (Example: Seaming the front and back of a sweater together.)

1. With a threaded tapestry needle and RS of the pieces to be joined facing up and laid parallel to each other, insert the needle into the first stitch on the right-hand side. Scoop the bar in between the "v" of your stitch. Repeat this on the left hand side of your work.

2. Continue in this manner on every seam, working loosely. Pull taut every inch (3 cm) or so.

Backstitch:

The backstitch seam is very strong and durable, but will form a ridge. It's a good seam for bags, or if you want to hide two less-than-perfect edges.

1. With a threaded tapestry needle and RS of the pieces to be joined facing each other, pin the corners together, matching the pieces up as closely as possible.

2. Secure the seam by taking the needle, front to back, twice around the edges of fabric.

3. Take the yarn around the outside edge once more, this time inserting the needle through the work from back to front, a little ahead of where the yarn last came out.

4. Insert the needle from front to back where the last stitch began, then bring the needle back through the front, maintaining the same distance between stitches.

5. Repeat steps 3 and 4 along the entire seam. Secure the end with two overlapping stitches.

Whipstitch:

This isn't exactly a pretty stitch, but it's fine to use on sections that won't be visible. It's also fun to incorporate into a finished design, such as using a contrasting yarn color to seam a pillow.

1. Place the pieces to be seamed together with edges lined up. Insert a threaded tapestry needle into the edge of the work from back to front and pull through.

Repeat at ¼-inch (½-cm) intervals along the entire seam.

SINGLE CROCHET (sc)

This stitch can be worked either off the crochet chain or off of a knit edge.

For working off the crochet chain:

1. Insert hook into the second loop of the crochet chain. Bring yarn over the hook front through back, and pull hook back through loop (you now have two loops on your hook).

2. Bring the yarn over your hook, again back to front, and pull through both loops on the hook.

3. Repeat steps 1 and 2 for the entire row.

To work the single crochet on a knit edge, work steps 1 and 2, but there is no need to skip the first stitch in the row.

SLIP, SLIP, KNIT DECREASE (ssk)

This decrease creates a left slant in your finished item.

1. Slip 2 stitches knit-wise, one at a time, from the left-hand needle to the right-hand needle.

2. Insert the left needle into the front of both slipped stitches and knit them together.

SLIP, SLIP, PURL DECREASE (ssp)

1. Slip 2 stitches knit-wise, one at a time, from the left-hand needle to the right-hand needle.

2. Slip both stitches back to the left needle.

3. Purl both stitches together through the back loop.

STOCKINETTE (OR STOCKING) STITCH (St st)

Unlike the garter stitch or rib stitch, the Stockinette stitch always has a front side and a back side. It's created by knitting one row, then purling the next row. The front will almost always be your knit side, and the back your purl side.

WEAVING IN ENDS

There is really no right way or wrong way to weave, as long as your finished work is secure and the woven threads do not show. It's best to experiment to find out what works for you. *Note: If you don't have a tapestry needle, a crochet hook can work just as well.*

1. Thread tail to be woven through tapestry needle.

2. Weave on wrong side of work, horizontally, making sure to stretch fabric occasionally so it does not gather. Take care to alternate the direction you insert your needle.

: RESOURCES

Araucania Nature Wool
www.araucaniayarns.com
US: Knitting Fever Inc.
          www.knittingfever.com
          (516) 546-3600
Canada: Diamond Yarn
          www.diamondyarn.com

Bernat
www.bernat.com
(888) 368-8401

Berroco Inc.
www.berroco.com
(508) 278-2527

Caron
www.caron.com

Cascade Yarns
www.cascadeyarns.com

Cushendale Worsted Weight Yarn
www.abbeyyarns.com

DMC embroidery thread
www.dmc-usa.com
(973) 589-0606

Knit Picks
www.knitpicks.com
(800) 574-1323

Lion Brand Yarns
www.lionbrand.com
(800) 661-7551

Patons Yarns
www.patonsyarns.com
(888) 368-8401

Plymouth Yarn
www.plymouthyarn.com
(215) 788-0459

Stitch Nation Yarn
www.stitchnationyarn.com

HOT CELEBRITY NERD ALERT!

Vin Diesel plays the game *Dungeons & Dragons*. For the film *xXx*, he had a fake tattoo of his D&D character's name put onto his stomach!